# The Mystery and Meaning of Christian Conversion

## George E. Morris

Prepared under the Direction of
The World Methodist Council

Discipleship Resources          Nashville

Scripture quotations noted RSV are from the Revised Standard Version of the Bible, copyrighted 1946, 1952, 1957. Quotations noted KJV are from the King James Version. All other quotations are from the New English Bible, © the Delegates of the Oxford University and the Syndics of the Cambridge University Press, 1961, 1970.

EV127B

*TO BARBARA*

# CONTENTS

# Foreword

Professor George Morris has written the most significant book on Christian conversion which has appeared for many years. It is a scholarly presentation, yet is written in a way which opens its truth to a wide audience of readers. It will especially appeal to pastors and thoughtful lay persons around the world.

The book begins where theological reflection and interpretation should begin, with what God is doing in human lives. The opening story of the conversion of Dr. Morris himself lays the foundation for many of the insights that follow. His understanding of conversion has been further enlightened by his ministry in local churches and his years of leadership in evangelism through the Board of Discipleship of The United Methodist Church. His insights have been further clarified and strengthened through his teaching ministry as Professor of Evangelism at the Candler School of Theology in Atlanta, Georgia.

Ever since Saul of Tarsus became Paul the Christian and Augustine the sensualist became Augustine the saint, the Christian church has been unable to forget the reality of the transforming power of Jesus Christ. In a world which is being threatened by raw, unredeemed human nature, and where millions of people know little or nothing of the Christian faith, conversion becomes central to the proclamation of the gospel. As the church, again with greater urgency, reaches outward to people who live perpetually beyond the influence of the Christian faith, it needs to have its own faith strengthened and its understanding deepened regarding what happens when men and women become reconciled to God through Jesus Christ. Hence Dr. Morris is, in these pages, offering a most timely book.

The whole Christian church needs to be recalled to belief in conversion. For decades the so-called liberal church has neglected the reality of conversion. The more conservative churches have made much of being "born again," yet all too often they reveal a limited understanding of what it means to enter fully into the new life of Christ.

*The Mystery and Meaning of Christian Conversion* presents conversion in the breadth and depth of its significance. Drawing heavily on Wesleyan evangelical theology, it shows how the Holy Spirit prepares people for the moment of conversion and the way in which the miracle of changed lives occurs. It brings together the two vital elements which must be present in any true conversion: a new relationship with God, and a new neighborly commitment. It shows how the personal and the social aspects of the gospel belong together in all true evangelism.

The World Evangelism Committee of The World Methodist Council invited Dr. Morris to write *The Mystery and Meaning of Christian Conversion*. It is proud to present this book, believing it will become an important resource for the whole Christian church. It will be especially valuable to the new World Evangelism Institute, which the Fourteenth World Methodist Conference, meeting in Hawaii in July 1981, agreed should be established. Dr. Morris has been appointed as the Director of the Institute, which is to be related to the Candler School of Theology at Emory University in Atlanta, Georgia. With great confidence the World Evangelism Committee sends forth this important book, praying that it will strengthen the evangelical witness of the church throughout the world.

ALAN WALKER
Director of World Evangelism
for The World Methodist Council

Sydney, Australia

# Acknowledgments

I am grateful to the authors and publishers whose works are cited for permission to quote from their works. I am especially grateful to those teachers, students, authors, pastors, and friends whose ideas have slipped into my own consciousness and may have surfaced here as my own. I have been helped by so many that I could never acknowledge all who have informed my thinking.

Before mentioning those to whom I have been more directly indebted in the preparation of this material, I must pause to salute the memory of two mentors whose influence upon me has been determinative. It was the late Dr. Harry Denman who brought me into the mainstream of evangelism ministries and held before me the challenge tirelessly to offer Christ to a desperate world. The late Dr. George Outen constantly stimulated me with his balanced view of personal and social salvation. My association with these brothers in Christ helped to shape the focus and style of all the evangelism ministries I have attempted to date.

In connection with this particular publication, I have to thank Dr. Alan Walker, Dr. Joe Hale, and Dean Jim Waits without whose encouragement I would never have attempted to write this book. My special thanks go to Dr. Theodore Runyon, my colleague here at Candler School of Theology. He read the manuscript and provided excellent encouragement and advice. Ms. Rebecca Short Burgess and my wife, Barbara, have rendered valuable assistance in typing the manuscript. My students, former parishioners, and fellow pastors have provided a sounding board for the testing of most of the ideas found in this book. I thank them one and all.

The questions at the end of each chapter have been added by

the publisher. They will suggest areas for further probing by the individual reader or in chapter-by-chapter study of this book by a group.

The following discussion of Christian conversion is deliberately theological. I do, however, hope and pray that it will be so intertwined with the realities of human existence that conversion can be seen for what it is: God's answer to human need.

George E. Morris
Candler School of Theology

# Introduction: In the Beginning

I was born and reared in a part of the United States called Southern Appalachia. My father worked with a coal company, and I spent the first seventeen years of my life in coal camps in the southwestern mountains of Virginia. During my formative years our home was not a Christian home. To the contrary, my consciousness of religion was shaped by a definite skepticism that rooted deeply in my family. To the best of my knowledge this skepticism dated back to my grandfather who was a medical doctor. He had read the writings of Robert Ingersoll and was convinced that religion was mainly superstition. This skepticism grew increasingly rigid, and during the final decade of my grandfather's life, from what I have been able to discover, he had become a militant atheist.

When my father was six years of age my grandfather left my grandmother and the children without food and fuel in a very remote region of Southern Appalachia. They would have perished had it not been for my father's oldest brother who learned of their predicament, hitched a sled to a team of horses, crossed the mountain in the dead of winter, and brought my grandmother and the children back to a region in Virginia called Poor Valley. There they survived the rest of the winter in a small mountain shack. Thus, my father grew up in the coal fields. He started working in the mines when he was sixteen years old and finally worked his way up to shipping clerk. My mother and father had eleven children, but only four of the eleven are living today. I was their seventh son.

When I was in high school a Methodist pastor moved into our

region. His name was Herndon Shepherd. He knew that we were not Christians and began to show a special interest in my father. He would visit my father from time to time and did his best to show his love for the whole family. Though my father did not admit it at the time, later on he was able to say that even in those early visits he had the profoundest respect for the pastor. When I was a senior in high school, Reverend Shepherd invited an evangelist to his church to conduct a series of meetings. They came down to the local high school to hold an assembly program. I cannot remember anything about that program except a chorus which we were taught. It went: "Everybody Ought to Know Who Jesus Is." During the assembly, as Reverend Shepherd looked out over the audience, he said the Lord spoke to his heart and told him to visit my father as soon as possible. In obedience, he went to visit my father at Blue Diamond Coal Company. He told my father that it was his responsibility to see that his two teenage children attended services at the church that week. When my father came home from work that evening he announced, "Get ready, we're going to church tonight."

I shall never forget my first impression of that meeting. We arrived late for the service, and when we entered the sanctuary it seemed to me that every person in the church was looking at us. When the evangelist rose to preach he told about a woman who had been turned to salt. He kept telling us to "remember Lot's wife." I didn't know Lot or his wife! I was conscious of the fact that he was trying to scare me and I was determined not to allow it. These are the only impressions that I can recall. To be honest, I spent most of my time talking with a classmate sitting next to me and aggravating the teenage girls in the pew ahead of us.

The next thing I remember distinctly is the image of my own father kneeling at the front of that church and the sound of his voice as he earnestly wept. Before long my mother was kneeling beside him. I can remember burning with embarrassment and wanting to get out of there and run like the wind. At the same time I leaned forward with curiosity wondering what would happen next. At about that moment my father stood, turned around, and started up the center aisle. Though I had never seen this done before, intuitively, I knew that he was coming for me. I crawled across the people standing next to me and went all the way against the wall, but my father pursued me. He put his arm on my shoulder and whispered words that changed the whole direction of my life. He said, "Son, I know this is embarrassing to you, but I want you to hear me out. I have found something here this evening that I have been searching for for fifty-six years, and I would rather die than see you make the mistake I have made." I said, "Well, what do you want me to do?" "Go down there," he said. Believe it or not, I did!

When I reached the front of the church I knelt exactly where my mother and father had knelt. An elderly woman named Mrs. Evans came, knelt beside me, and shared the simple message of the gospel. She said, "Son, did you know that God loves you?" I said, "No, ma'am." She said, "Why son, he loves you so much that he sent his Son to die for you. Do you believe that?" I said, "Mrs. Evans, is that what my father believes?" She responded, "That's what your father believes." I answered, "Then I will believe it, too." She said, "Will you commit your life to God?" I said, "Mrs. Evans, I don't know what you mean by that." "That means that your life is not going to be just yours anymore, you are giving your life to God." I responded, "Is that what my father did?" "That's what your father did," she said. And I said, "Then I will do it too."

Now at that moment something happened in my life that I have never been able to fully understand or articulate. However, one deep impression was imprinted on my mind and heart. I was suddenly overcome with a deep sense of compassion for everyone in that place. I wanted to reach out and embrace them all, and my heart was so filled with joy and gratitude that I felt I could not contain it. Keith Miller has given expression to what I felt that night and the days immediately following. According to Miller, there follows for the convert,

A strange awareness that he has entered a whole new segment of his life—as if he had turned a page and begun a new chapter. . . . The recently converted Christian . . . wants to become different from his past. . . . He is highly motivated to learn a whole new style of living. . . . His horizons have expanded, along with the possibilities of what he may become as a loving person. His old dominant values . . . don't seem important as compared to learning about God and His will in ordinary life. . . . The inner feeling is one of joy and gratitude.[1]

After returning home that night, my mind began immediately to reflect upon the mystery and the meaning of this event. I talked with my mother for several hours and I recall that it was she who first introduced me to the word *conversion*.

## THE CONTEXT

I have found it impossible to write a book on Christian conversion without reference to my own experience. I realize that one must be careful in beginning a book in such a way. This is especially true if one's story is one of dramatic Christian conversion. Many Christians are driven to the mistaken conclusion that they are not converted because they cannot find anything in their religious pilgrimage which is remotely similar to the stories of dramatic conversion. In telling my own story I am not insinuating that the reader's experience must coincide with mine.

I have told my own story because of the conviction that Christian conversion cannot be understood apart from one's cultural context. Conversion always takes place within a particular historical culture, and it does not extract a person from his or her inherited cultural matrix, nor does it mean an automatic denial of all of one's past life. Thus, my purpose in telling my own story is to offset the attempt to view Christian conversion as a transcultural noncontextual event. This noncontextual view opens up the possibility of a more devastating error—that of assuming that Christian conversion happens to all believers, everywhere, at the same point in life, and in the same way. It will be the purpose of this book to view Christian conversion as a dynamic, complex, ongoing process which is greatly impacted by particular times and places and considerably shaped by contexts. I will attempt to show how Christian conversion takes places at the intersection of God's way and our ways.

Since I was not brought up in the Christian faith, my own conversion contained a radicality that is not always present for a person who has known intentional Christian nurture. For instance, the issue of continuity and discontinuity was immediately forced to the forefront of my consciousness. I learned that I had to abandon behavior that had been perfectly acceptable, at least to me, before my conversion. I found myself having to accept behavioral patterns that were prevalent among the majority of our small congregation. For example, I soon learned that dancing was considered sinful by the leaders of my local church. Though I never really believed this, I did my best to conform to their expected norms. After four or five months I began to sense that this new community of people was laying hard demands on me, demands that tended to disregard my past life.

In retrospect, I now see that I was expected to exhibit Christian virtues that one might find in a full-grown mature Christian rather than a newborn baby in Christ. This lack of respect for the continuity of past and present was characteristic of the revivalist structures into which I was spiritually born. There was an attempt to force radical discontinuity with one's past—as if one could suddenly wipe away the first seventeen years of life and all the accumulated old habits. I often felt that God, in fashioning a new creation, was expected to embroider in the empty air rather than on an existing piece of material.

Moreover, as a new Christian, I had to learn "old" hymns, and I found myself constantly struggling to understand what the preacher meant by words and phrases in his sermons. Fortunately, I was eager to learn and did not hesitate to ask questions. The people were always kind and willing to take the time to share with me.

Shortly after my conversion, Reverend Shepherd helped me understand the need for Christian baptism and church membership. Therefore, from the very beginning of my Christian pilgrimage I was able to see the intimate connection between baptism and conversion. He taught me that Christian baptism was a kind of seal or symbol of the new relationship with God which comes as a gift of the Holy Spirit and through which one is initiated into the fellowship of the church. He explained to me the three modes of baptism practiced in the Wesleyan tradition. However, since immersion was the most popular mode practiced in our area, I chose to be immersed in a small river in the hills of Southern Appalachia. This was a great experience for me, and it did in fact signal the beginning of a new life and a new relationship. On that same Sunday I was received into the membership of the church.

There were positive evidences that something unusual had happened in my life. There was a basic change of attitude; that is, I wanted to love people. There were also concrete acts of compassion and witness. I remember telling my mother that I was both surprised and somewhat confused by this new and mysterious compassion that made me want to reach out to people. To my family's great surprise I did not hesitate to tell anyone who would listen (and some who would not) that I had been converted to Jesus Christ and that I had begun a new life. No one had to force me to pray, study scripture, and attend church. I wanted to! In only a short time I had read the entire New Testament. Though I often found the readings terribly confusing, nevertheless, at times glimmers came through and I learned to expect God's divine disclosure through the scriptures. My participation in the local church helped me understand that I was more than a solitary individual interested only in my own well-being. I began to see that I could contribute to the well-being and enrichment of others.

## THE MEANING AND THE MYSTERY

This is the first time that I have endeavored to put my own conversion experience into writing. I have found it impossible to give an exact reconstruction of the events that took place during my seventeenth year. However, after consulting with members of The Methodist Church at the time, I do feel confident that this is an accurate description.

From the beginning I have been inclined to believe that much of Christian conversion remains in the realm of mystery. It is one thing to try to give an accurate description of an experience, but it is something else to try to get at the meaning of that experience. This does not mean that there is nothing we can know about Christian conversion. It simply means that we cannot adequately answer every question raised. I can only confess to the reader that I have spent a lifetime trying to decipher the mystery and meaning of Christian conversion. I say "a lifetime" because these events during my seventeenth year were the beginning of a long process that has not ended.

It is my purpose in this book to show that Christian conversion is, in fact, an ongoing process, even though the beginnings of that process are both discernible and consequential. Moreover, it will be my purpose to go behind human experience itself and probe the meaning and the mystery of God's action in our lives. Thus the primary focus of this book will be an attempt to think theologically about Christian conversion. I am aware that it is impossible to make an absolute distinction between experience and theology. The two definitely interpenetrate and impact one another. Nevertheless, this interpenetration must not be overstated. There is a real difference between experience and theological interpretation.[2]

## QUESTIONS FOR THOUGHT AND DISCUSSION

1. The author begins with the story of his own conversion. You too may wish to begin this study by writing down and sharing the story of critical turning points in your Christian journey.

2. In the author's conversion what is the role played by past generations? By his immediate family? By the pastor? The

evangelist? The congregation? The Bible? God? What functions do these play in your own story?

3. Conversion is understood here as happening in a specific "context" of personal and cultural influences, "at the intersection between God's ways and our ways." Describe the context of one conversion experience you know well, your own or another person's.

# 1. Christian Conversion in Theological Perspective

This book intends to be a positive affirmation of the conversion experience. But it is more than that. Too often books and articles on conversion focus on the conversion experience *as experience*. Such an approach can lead to a number of pitfalls. First, it can treat conversion solely as an object of research. It is assumed that we can predict and control any human experience once we have broken it down into parts and analyzed it. Giving in to our propensity for managing and analyzing, we attempt to take the conversion experience apart in order to study each phase in minute detail. Once these phases are delineated it is assumed that conversion can be completely understood.

I am not implying that it is illegitimate to analyze Christian conversion. I am merely saying that analysis has severe limitations. But dissecting a profound Christian conversion is like attempting to hold a moonbeam in your hand. The mystery is often so deep that it is inexplicable, and our puny categories cannot exhaust the meaning there. No one can hope to encompass in word and thought the mystery and meaning of Christian conversion in all its concrete actuality. For in this experience one is confronted with the ultimate mystery in which the love of God lays hold upon the mind, heart, and conscience of a human being. As H. H. Farmer affirms: "If God thus encounters and deals with us in Christ, well then, so he encounters and deals with us, and behind that it is not possible to go to anything deeper and more ultimate." [1] We deceive ourselves when we think we can dissect Christian conversion and describe it in detail.

Another pitfall in an exaggerated concentration on experience is the temptation to make human experience the final arbiter of the gospel. Persons or groups who fall into this trap tend to assume that anyone is a Christian as long as he or she *feels* religious. Rather than the content of the gospel being the final authority and content by which the experience is judged, the experience itself becomes a prior standard by which we accept or reject the gospel's claims. Therefore, the gospel must submit and be tried by the code of human experience rather than the reverse, and the appeal to experience is divorced from the historical revelation of God in Christ. This leads to a general appeal to vague, spiritual emotions which might make us feel religious in the general sense of the word, but will not necessarily make us Christian. Christian conversion is more than a comfortable, genial, religious feeling which scarcely penetrates the surface of one's life. As we shall see, Christian conversion goes to the depths.

In Christian conversion it is not our experience that interprets the Christ but *the Christ who interprets our experience*. If we use our experience to interpret the gospel of Christ, then Christ ceases to be sovereign, and our religious experience becomes the criterion for authentic Christian conversion. But it must be the other way around. Christ and the gospel must be the criterion of our experience. We must be accountable to the gospel rather than making the gospel accountable to us. When our human experience becomes the criterion we tend to give a limited response to the unlimited grace of God. We attempt to dictate to God the terms of conversion. We say, "Yes, Lord, I will follow you so long as you are going my way." The Christian life becomes a pilgrimage with provisos written in. We say, "This is where our paths part; this is as far as we go; this is where we get off!"

Even more serious, there are those who attempt to compel Christ to go their way. They then proceed to chart their own course in the name of their captive Christ. They clothe Christ in the cast-iron armor of their own ideas and experiences rather than having their lives centered in Christ. This Christ, who is the captive to experiences, can be stripped of his seamless robe and wrapped in the cape and hood of the Ku Klux Klan. He can be dressed in the three-piece suit of a laissez-faire capitalist. He can be shoved before a television camera or out into the streets to advertise all sorts of bright ideas and fads. This captive Christ can be conscripted and issued the ill-fitting uniform of almost any nation or group fighting for almost any "cause." Christ can be dolled up and sentimentalized. All his "hard sayings" can be washed from his mouth with soft soap.

Indeed it is dangerous to frame an understanding of Christian conversion solely upon the basis of human experience!

Now, certainly this is not an attempt to disregard or belittle the place of experience in Christian conversion. The affective (or emotional) aspect of conversion must be affirmed in an age that hungers for experience. I am simply refusing to give the affective aspect first position. I choose to begin at the point of the gospel of Jesus Christ. I will attempt to view Christian conversion in theological perspective.

## BRINGING THE GOSPEL TO BEAR

To view Christian conversion in theological perspective means that all Christian doctrines, as well as subjective experiences, must be brought under the close scrutiny of the gospel. The gospel is utterly normative. If my personal story of faith is authentic, then it will confirm the key events and perceptions in the Story of Christ (the gospel). Moreover, my experience must get its bearings from the gospel. When this process is reversed, distortions are inevitable. So my purpose will be to bring the gospel to bear on our understanding of Christian conversion, realizing that without theological clarity conversion falls into the pit of pure subjective experience and evangelism falls into disrepute.

Bringing the gospel to bear on conversion must not be confused with providing a theology *for* Christian conversion. Such an enterprise would tend to degenerate into producing on demand a coherent, rational, foolproof theological justification for what is self-evident to a particular group. This is a popular way of "doing" theology. As a result, in the current bill-of-fare we are provided with "theologies" of sex, of body, of revolution, of joy—and the list goes on and on. Leander Keck points out that "the ancients had gods for different functions and activities like war, sex, justice, order, emotions, agriculture, navigation, and the like. Gods were specialists. In the same way, we have developed special interest gods each of whom has his or her own theology—to say nothing of cult." [2] Each of these so-called theologies is designed to justify an emphasis, a point of view, or a program of action and reads the whole of Christian theology through the peephole of its particular platform or project.

This transformation of theology into ideology robs theology of its self-critical function, and the theologian becomes a propagandist, a lobbyist for a point of view.[3] Accordingly, one's affirmation of faith and one's ambitions are carefully joined. Even Jesus's own image gets terribly diluted because of its associations with causes that people wish to justify. Bruce Reed says,

> For many [Jesus] has been stripped of his messianic authority and emptied of his sense of mission, so that like a golliwog he is filled up with notions which someone wants to justify; he becomes a guerilla fighter, say, or a homosexual. A stage has been reached where people reading the gospels for the first time react negatively against the Jesus portrayed there, and reject the image of God he offers.[4]

This is inevitable when Jesus is used to justify our causes and programs.

Moreover, when we use theology to justify an emphasis, God becomes an object to be manipulated to our own selfish advantage. Keck says,

> Whenever God is regarded simply as the reality that guarantees who we are or want to be, God has been turned into an ideological warrant. Such a God has no freedom to come or go, no freedom to build up or tear down, to reveal or to hide. Such a God can be real only if our projects prosper and our experiences of him are positive. Such a God, of course, would never show up on a cross.[5]

Suffice it to say, theology should not be used to justify an experience or to buttress a point of view or to sell a program.

On the other hand, bringing the gospel to bear on the nature of Christian conversion means involving ourselves in a critical assessment; allowing the light of the gospel to illumine, assess, and where necessary, correct our experiences. In saying that theology grows out of the good news of Jesus Christ I am not insinuating that theology is a seamless garment of infallible systematic answers to the human situation. This mistake has led to the reduction of the gospel to propositions and doctrines, or an attempt to obtain the substance of salvation in dogmatics. I am merely asserting that the process of Christian conversion is given form and consciousness through the theological rationale, which contains, molds, and is vitalized by it. When experience becomes the final arbiter, this tends to dislocate the place of the Christian gospel. What gospel there is left falls prey to innumerable sweetenings and adaptations which denature Christianity by adjusting it to our own wants and desires. Ultimately, the Christian message loses its saltiness and becomes sugary.

In addition, it is necessary to speak of Christian conversion in theological perspective because there are so many kinds of conversion. As a result of this confusion, Christian conversion tends to lose its clear profile. The lines are so blurred that it is no longer easy to identify clearly what Christian conversion really is. For this reason the Christian must struggle to find criteria for identifying Christian conversion, criteria which are both authentic and viable. This attempt will lead us to concentrate upon the normative position of the gospel of Jesus Christ. But first it will be necessary to take a closer look at the current situation that confronts us.

## QUESTIONS FOR THOUGHT AND DISCUSSION

1. The author describes some dangers in focusing solely on the experience itself as we try to understand conversion. What are these dangers and what others would you add?

2. What does he mean, "It is not our experience that interprets the Christ but the Christ who interprets our experience" (p. 10). Give examples of each from your own life.

3. What is the difference between bringing conversion under the scrutiny of the gospel and merely developing a theological justification for conversion (pp. 11-13)? Illustrate each.

# 2. The Modern Babel

There is a great confusion of tongues regarding the meaning of Christian conversion and the code words used to talk about conversion. These words carry a lot of negative baggage in the minds of people. Nor is this a new development. The problem has been around for a long time. However, today the problem presents itself with increasing intensity. The examples of this confusion are legion.

I was invited to preach in a large United Methodist church in the northeastern part of the United States. After the worship service, the pastor and I were standing in the narthex greeting the people as they left the sanctuary. Up stepped a well-dressed man in his middle forties. His hair was curly blonde and he was strong in stature. His pastor introduced him as Dr. So-and-so. The man gripped my hand firmly and said, "Well, this wasn't what I expected it to be!" I braced myself and waited for the worst. He continued, "Actually, I enjoyed every minute of it. If I'm not on call at the hospital this evening, I'd like to come back again. What will your subject be this evening?" After a moment's thought, I said, "I plan to speak on conversion." His demeanor changed immediately and he said, "Oh, good Lord! I thought we had left that back in the days of sawdust trails and holy rollers!"

During a recent flight to a midwestern city I sat beside a woman who was reading a copy of *Newsweek*. The article and cover story were titled "Born Again Politics." As a conversation starter I asked what she thought of the article. She responded, "The more I read about born-again Christians, the more confused I get. I get the impression that being 'born-again' gives a person a religious reason for holding to a right-wing political position. It seems that 'born-again' and 'narrow-minded' are synonymous."

I have encountered similar opinions all over the United States and in different parts of the world. These views indicate that some of the Christian community's most important words have fallen into disrepute. A set of interpretations has been fastened on some of our essential words obscuring their original meaning in the scripture, misrepresenting the character of Christian evangelism, and often alienating church members as well as outsiders.

Of all the words in the Christian vocabulary, few will get a more immediate response than the word *conversion*. Both inside and outside the church, people react positively or negatively—and often heatedly!—at the very mention of the term. The word seems to conjure up all kinds of images.

On several occasions, in different parts of the world, I have conducted word-association exercises with groups of lay persons and clergy. These exercises have taught me that I dare not assume a positive reaction when using important words in the Christian's vocabulary. In computing the results of these exercises I discovered the following: When some people think of conversion they think of a highly emotional experience often accompanied by weeping and moaning and rolling on the floor. Most people are quick to say that they want nothing to do with such an emotional upheaval—at least not in church. At a ball game or party maybe, but church is much too "nice" a place for such behavior. When others hear the word used they think of a process by which one preserves one's immortal soul for its final destiny to another world. This seems to be so otherworldly as to be of no earthly good. Thus conversion is dismissed as totally irrelevant.

The results from outsiders are not any more encouraging. When those outside the church hear the word *conversion*, they might have some remote or vague notion relating conversion to a huge auditorium, tent, or stadium. Some remember being buttonholed by a stranger with the question, "Brother, sister, are you saved?" Is it any wonder that mainstream Christianity has felt uncomfortable with the word *conversion*?

But beyond a doubt, along with confusion, we are experiencing a new interest in conversion. This interest is being generated by a number of current developments.

## QUEST FOR EXPERIENCE

First, there is the quest for experience. In today's world people are actively seeking religious experience. They are searching for a "word from beyond." They want to sense a transcendent reality. Everywhere we turn there are symptoms of this quest. In the burgeoning phenomena of new fundamentalism, new pentecostalism, and new evangelical movements, we see symptoms of a great spiritual hunger. Some of the members of our churches are defecting to these movements because they say mainline denominations have so protected themselves against the invasion of the Spirit that they can no longer experience God there.

We see symptoms of this quest in the rapid growth of non-Christian movements. People's quest for transcendence is causing them to take a new look at all kinds of non-Christian sources. Therefore, they flock to the occult, experiment with all forms of ancient superstitions, and turn to eastern mysticism. It may be that people read astrological charts more than they read the holy scriptures.

A growing dissatisfaction with technology is another symptom. People are learning that "getting the goods" and "feeling good" are not mutually inclusive. As Jacques Ellul argues, the price of our technocracy has been a greater dependence upon the artificiality of the technical society which dominates our lives.[1] However, today, people have experienced the limits of our materialistic wonders and are beginning to look elsewhere for meaning.

This dissatisfaction with technology is linked with a dangerous impatience with reason, an impatience which encourages people to dispense with understanding and concentrate solely on "feeling it in the heart." But one can understand this reaction if one takes into account what has been happening in our world for several years. Part of the reason for the current hunger for religious experience comes from the fact that, for some time now, many educators and pastors have gone about their task as if people were only minds. This has been true not only in our public schools but in our churches. An overemphasis on cognition and thinking has tended to present the Christian faith as a set of facts that must be learned. Instead of seeing human life as a whole pattern of thinking, feeling, and willing, we have viewed life and learning more in terms of the accumulation of information and ideas. This has tended to downplay the important role of human affection and emotion, and even hold them suspect. John Westerhoff contends that throughout our life we need to *experience* faith. "Experience is foundational to faith. A person first learns Christ not as a theological affirmation but as an affective experience." [2]

In addition, this quest for experience can also be seen in an insatiable desire for community. People are linking themselves with all sorts of groups and movements that are supposed to enable them to experience shared meanings. They ride every bandwagon available hoping to satisfy their deep longings for experience, but often wind up more empty and alone than when they started.

This quest for experience is worldwide and it touches every sector of life. We see it among the rich and the poor, in the affluent suburbs and in the low-rent sections of the innercity. We see it on our campuses, in the military, and every other place. So predominant is this quest for experience that one writer claims that despite the theological and sociological variety in the current movements, the "one thing which characterizes them all is a search for, and reported rediscovery of, what is variously called the presence of God." [3] On the basis of his research, John Biersdorf claims that the hunger for experience is descriptive of the growing edge of religion. [4] So great is this hunger that people "consume" experiences and meanings, choosing between meaning symbols in much the same way as consumers choose products in the marketplace. [5] Biersdorf concludes, "When a culture becomes fragmented and confused, as is ours, people hunger for experience to help them integrate their lives and find strength for living." [6] They "feel a need for authentic personal experience and close interpersonal relationships to restore meaning to their lives." [7]

This questing for experience makes the task of viewing conversion in theological perspective even more imperative, lest our people settle for the experience itself and spurn the gospel, the only legitimate criterion for Christian conversion. The call is not to suppress one in order to highlight the other but to get the two into perspective. We cannot, however, take up this task at all until we confront the challenge of people's hunger for experience.

In the face of this challenge, Peter Berger issues a stunning forecast: "If Christianity has a future, it will be in the resurgence of Christian experience and faith in the lives of people." [8] Denominational leaders, pastors, theologians and leading laypersons desperately need to hear this word. For instead of interpreting this quest for experience as a signal from our world calling us to our true vocation of furnishing occasions for living in the presence of God, those of us in places of leadership in the church have tended to insulate ourselves from these needs by concentrating more intently on institutional maintenance. Because leaders in mainline churches have shied away from the task of encouraging and interpreting Christian experience, this realm has been left largely to charismatics, mystics, followers of Eastern disciplines, and humanistic psychologists. Not only are some leaders ill-equipped to deal with those who quest for experience, but many show an alarming lack of interest in it.

Now I am not arguing that religious experiences are less frequent. People are incurably religious. They are religious by nature. They will worship something. To my mind, it is incorrect to think of people as "irreligious." People are never "irreligious," they are only "other religious." Wherever we find people—no matter what their cultural environment, no matter what their history—they are seeking transcendence. They worship; they call out to powers beyond themselves; they are very religious. To the contrary, I am arguing that it is precisely our unwillingness to recognize this quest that is producing a revival of bizarre expressions of religious consciousness. When our hunger for the experience of transcendence is repressed, all kinds of countering influences come to the surface.

One would expect that the worldwide Wesleyan family, of all

people, would be responsive to this quest for religious experience. In our past, experiential response to the gospel was accepted as normative. However, it seems that churches in the Wesleyan tradition have come to mirror the rest of secular society. Secularization has declared the experience of transcendence which involves the heart to be rated X.[9] One gets the impression that the church has followed suit. For some time there has been an attempt to repress the consciousness and experience of transcendence. At times this attempt is overt and deliberate, at other times covert and subtle.

Joe Hale, General Secretary of The World Methodist Council, gives a graphic illustration of how church leaders attempt to repress the experience of transcendence. He tells of a teenager, who in the exhilaration of her newfound faith, exclaimed to her pastor, "I have had an experience with Christ." That teenager was made to feel embarrassed and met with the response, "Not you? You are a fine Christian and have always been a member of the church. An experience with Christ is reserved for those outside the church who need to be converted." Hale acknowledges that this is the kind of repression which takes place when either the society or the church says "Your experience (what you are telling me) is not legitimate." When we refuse to affirm persons who have opened their lives to God and experienced grace, we may be creating a substantial obstacle to the Spirit's work.[10]

It is because the living God is not a present reality to us that our witness has lost its force. People tend to ossify and become sterile without up-to-date experiences of transcendence. Paul Tournier tells this story:

I have had a close friendship with a group of French pastors who conducted evangelistic missions with wholehearted zeal in various parishes. After one of these, they were received, in the late evening, by one of the notables of the parish. The latter was expressing his enthusiasm for the spiritual message they had brought. He added: "As a matter of fact, I, too, have had a religious experience." And turning to his wife, he said, "Would you mind going up to the attic and getting it? You remember, I wrote it out and framed it. It must be in the big chest at the far end. These gentlemen would be interested to see it." A moment later the wife came back with the famous religious experience under her arm, but she had to beg pardon for producing it in such a condition, because the rats had been at it and had left it in a lamentable state![11]

Can we really demonstrate in our lives that which is not a part of our personal experience? It is said that the early church turned the world upside down. That process has been reversed. Now it seems that the world is turning the church upside down. Why? I have the deep conviction that part of the reason is that inherited, secondhand, cold-storage concepts are proving inadequate for the living of these days. Voltaire once said of his relationship with Christ, "We salute, but we do not speak." This may be the problem of many in our churches. Many have grown up in a religious atmosphere that taught them to be polite to Christ. They salute Christ but they do not know him. They know about him but they do not know him. They have never experienced his love in their inmost being. Today, however, people are questing for God. They want to know God. This quest has succeeded in heightening both interest in and confusion about Christian conversion.

## THE MEDIA BOOM

Another current development which underlies both a new interest in and confusion about conversion is the resurgence of older evangelical groups and the emergence of new religious movements, many of which have been born out of mass media ministries. If the church does not acknowledge the power of the media, especially television, it will someday awaken to the realization that scores of people, who would otherwise have belonged to mainline churches, have now been "born again" out of television's experiential womb.

Professor Paul Kurtz, of the State University of New York, recently said that "a whole new generation of people are being confused and overwhelmed by the electronic media and are finding it increasingly difficult to distinguish fiction from reality." He went on to claim that this has caused a rapid growth of belief in the paranormal, the bizarre, and the occult. When many of these people are asked the source of their information they cite television shows that mix facts with fiction so cleverly that it is hard for people who are raised on television to sort things out. Kurtz contends that belief in the bizarre is furthered by the skillful use of propaganda. This is how occultism is sold to the gullible public. People are fascinated by it; it strikes their imagination and fancy. He concludes that people who need meaning and purpose in this rapidly changing and illogical world are getting their answers in the wrong places. For millions of Americans, the electronic media have replaced both the university and the church. The media have become sacred because they deal with the realm of imagination. As a result, critical judgment is being perverted and distorted. To illustrate his point Professor Kurtz tells the following story:

> I was in San Diego last year, and I was taken to a meeting hall which had been rented to a group of believers. Here were three hundred people, many of whom were holders of advanced college degrees, who believed in U.F.O.'s and creatures from outer space. A woman walked in who was dressed in a very strange costume and told everybody she was from Venus and that she communicated with our "space brothers" on outer spaceships. . . . I asked some of her disciples: "You don't really believe in this, do you? You know, the temperature is at least 800 degrees on Venus. Don't you think she'd burn?" They said: "No, no, no. You don't understand. She's on an ethereal plane."

Kurtz concludes that the electronic media are making it possible for anyone to believe anything.[12]

Many independent evangelical groups have seized the media as the prime means of advancing their cause. A recent issue of *Saturday Evening Post* carried an article titled, "The Gospel Boom." The writer enthused, "Snap on the T.V., turn up the stereo, pick up a paperback. Thanks to modern technology, the Christian message has been amplified. . . ." He went on to say that the entire "gospel industry"—from records to radio spots to best-selling books—is booming.[13] There are those who believe that this "gospel business," given its present power, is just on the launching pad and will skyrocket in the future.[14]

In this "gospel business" Jesus is being advertised, promoted, and marketed like any other consumer product. Thomas Merton is correct in observing:

> Popular religion has to a great extent betrayed man's inner spirit and turned him over, like Samson, with his hair cut off and his eyes dug out, to turn the mill of a self-frustrating and self-destroying culture. The clichés of popular religion have in many cases become every bit as hollow and as false as those of soap salesmen, and far more dangerously deceptive because one cannot so easily verify the claims made about the product. The sin of religiosity is that it has turned God, peace, happiness, salvation and all that man desires into products to be marketed in a speciously attractive package deal.[15]

This retailing of religion takes many forms but for the most part it operates on the axiom "the medium *is* the message." Therefore religion is hawked by the most advanced and manipulative means that are available. And Jesus is sold again for thirty pieces of silver!

There is an even more unfortunate mixing of means and ends. Mammon's means are used to achieve spiritual ends. Such a process insinuates that though salvation is free and comes by grace through faith, the presentation of the gospel is dependent upon clever and costly propaganda devices and techniques. In order to help the gospel "sell" it must be sugarcoated. As a result, the truth, precision, and authenticity of the Christian message is abased. Innumerable sweetenings and adaptations have resulted in the adulteration of the meaning of the gospel, the meaning of Christian conversion, and the Christian's code language (e.g., "born-again") used in speaking of the gospel and conversion.[16]

Perhaps the best example of the media's power is seen in the way in which the phrase *born-again* has been almost completely adulterated. The phrase is used as an adjective to describe almost anything. In its description of the growing media church the *Saturday Evening Post* employs the phrase "born-again airwaves" (p. 34). "Born-again Politics" was the caption on the front page of *Newsweek* (September 15, 1980). Born-again religion has become a popular cliché and is beginning to acquire a fairly consistent shape. The born-again experience is usually presented and understood as a guarantor of success, fame, prosperity, and respectability. Thus if you want to "make it" in this world, if you want to benefit from the primary cultural values and amenities, become a born-again Christian. The born-again experience is usually understood as a highly personalized matter which enables one to get ahead in this world, and thus the born-again syndrome fits beautifully into our secular culture. Since self-centeredness is a chief goal or value—that is, we want to be better adjusted, prosperous, and successful—conversion becomes the means to that end. When we invite Jesus into our lives, Jesus becomes "ours," and we use him for our own selfish purposes. So conversion happens only within individual selves and Jesus becomes another item that knowledgable consumers take into their lives for their own benefit and happiness. In this way the born-again experience is used to sanction and enhance the present order of things rather than calling it into question. Where could one find a better measure of the extent to which a prevailing cultural situation can distort into falsehood what the scriptures teach?

## SEMANTIC CONFUSION

Once every generation or so, the church must pause to ask the question: What is the meaning of Christian conversion? Because of current developments, I doubt if there has ever been a time when there has been greater confusion.

Part of this confusion regarding conversion comes from the fact that the word is not the exclusive property of the church. The term has fairly clearly defined technical meanings in the fields of theology, law, logic, mathematics, and psychology. It is often used in the empirical sciences to denote "change," "transformation," or "transposition." It is used in logic to denote a repositioning of the subject and predicate terms of a proposition. In law it means the assumption by one party of the rights over properties that belong to another.

To add to this confusion the word has several general meanings in the ordinary conversation of people. It can mean any change in a person's opinions or life orientation. For instance, the word can be used as a noun. We say, "She is a 'convert' to our way of thinking." It can also be used as a verb. For instance, we say, "I suspect that she was trying to convert me." That is, she was trying to get me to adopt a new point of view or to change my way of life.[17]

Conversion can also be used to denote change in a facet of one's life or it can mean a total reorientation. For instance, a person can be converted from stinginess to generosity in the management of money, or a student can be converted to realism with regard to political involvements. On the other hand, conversion can be spoken of in a much more radical fashion. It can mean transformation which is observed not so much in terms of a difference in this or that facet of a person's life, but a change so radical that the person becomes a new being.

A person can also be converted to non-Christian religions or anti-Christian political philosophies. The Bangkok Assembly admitted this when it said, "Conversion as a phenomenon is not restricted to the Christian community; it finds its place in other religions as well as in certain political and ideological communities."[18] William Sargant uses Arthur Koestler's conversion to communism to prove that mystical experiences, like sudden conversions, do not always arise from purely religious influences and stresses.[19] Koestler gives the following account of his conversion to communism:

Something clicked in my brain which shook me like a mental explosion. To say that one has seen the light is a poor description of the mental rapture which only the convert knows. The new light seems to pour from all directions across the skull; the whole universe falls into a pattern like the stray pieces of a jigsaw puzzle assembled by magic at one stroke. There is now an answer to every question.[20]

Sargant claims that experiences of this sort can be induced by a wide range of stresses on the brain. He says, "Feelings of divine possession, and subsequent conversion to a religious faith can be helped on by the use of many types of physiological stimuli." [21] Thus, conversion can be used to describe a political, economic, or social, as well as religious event. One can be converted to communism, the John Birch Society, or many other causes besides Christian faith. A person can even be converted to democracy. In no sense does the conversion in and of itself attest to the soundness of what you now espouse. Criteria other than one's own personal experience must be used to determine this.

For a number of years it has been popular to view conversion as a psychological phenomenon. Professor William James, as a result of his Gifford lectures in 1901-02, became the leading spokesman for this position. His lectures were later published in a book titled, *The Varieties of Religious Experience*. James ignored the institutional and ecclesiological aspects of religion and gave little consideration to theology. Rather, he concentrated on "personal religion pure and simple." From the vantage point he defined conversion in psychological language:

> To be converted, to be regenerated, to receive grace, to experience religion, to gain an assurance, are many phrases which denote the process, gradual or sudden, by which a self hitherto divided and consciously wrong, inferior and unhappy, becomes consciously right, superior and happy, in consequence of its firmer hold upon religious reality. This is at least what conversion signifies in general terms, whether or not we believe that a direct divine operation is needed to bring such a moral change about.[22]

As we can see, James' quest for scientific objectivity led him away from the conscious acknowledgment of theological presuppositions. Unfortunately, this schism between the theological and experiential has not been healed. Today, pastors and lay persons are faced with the unenviable choice of either reading systematic theologies that major on doctrinal suppositions and show little interest in or concern for the personal relations by which conversion might be accomplished, or else studies of personal, experiential conversion that contain no affirmations of faith or theological underpinning. Nevertheless, James' definition implies that, though a variety of terms is used to describe conversion, they are just "so many phrases" to describe a common phenomenon. He assumes that conversion can be spoken of in either supernatural or humanistic terms. Conversion may or may not be the result of "direct divine operation." James' definition of conversion has tended to be normative for the psychological approach.[23]

George Sweazey of Princeton admits that conversion can be a phenomenon that occurs when "a life that had no unifying center, or a different center, becomes organized around some dominating loyalty." However, Sweazey observes that a personality can be integrated at as low a level as, for instance, a passion for money. He says, "Any consuming interest can give a personality unity and force. . . . Hitler made converts. . . . To get organized around the right center is the life and death issue for everyone." [24] The primary focus of this book will not be upon such general understandings of conversion, but, quite specifically, upon the meaning of Christian conversion.

If the word *conversion* is confusing from the technical and general sense, it is equally confusing when understood as a purely religious word. In religious communities, there is no single phenomenon designated by the term *conversion,* but rather a cluster of phenomena. One discovers that a large number of fundamentally different experiences are loosely grouped under the word *conversion.* For example, it is sometimes used to denote the change that occurs when a person who has previously rejected religious beliefs accepts them once again. On the other hand, it can mean the change that occurs when a person who has always accepted Christian beliefs begins to take them seriously. As Lewis Rambo points out, to some it even means the transfer of membership from one denomination to another or the shift of loyalty from one religious tradition to a vastly different one.[25]

To add to this confusion there seems to be a contemporary distaste for the word. Because it and other words that depict Christian experience have been captured by narrow partisans, the word itself has become somewhat unpopular. This makes discussions of Christian conversion difficult because, "many people often believe that those involved in new religious movements must either be crazy to begin with or were brainwashed." [26] Some of this distaste is due to the fact that people who lay claim to conversion experiences often tend to adopt an air of superiority over those who have not.

This distaste for conversion can also be noted in the way the upper and middle classes tend to regard conversion as necessary only for the lower classes but hardly necessary for respectable folks like themselves. John R. W. Stott lists three reasons for discomfort with the term. First, it is rejected by some because of its association with that "dreadful phenomenon 'evangelical enthusiasm.' " Second, it is disliked because of the "impression of arrogant imperialism" which some evangelists have sometimes given. Evangelism can descend to the level of empire building, scalp hunting, or the numbers game. It is against these abuses that the Central Committee of the World Council of Churches aimed the following remark: "Witness is corrupted when cajolery, bribery, undue pressure or intimidation is used—subtly or openly—to bring about seeming conversions; when we put the success of our church before the honor of Christ; . . . when personal or corporate self-seeking replaces love for every individual soul for whom we are concerned. Such corruptions of the Christian witness indicate lack of confidence in the power of the Holy Spirit, lack of respect for the nature of man, lack of recognition of the true character of the gospel." [27]

If a sense of social inferiority and misguided forms of witness are two reasons for a distaste for conversion, Stott lists a third as "the doctrines of syncretism and universalism." Syncretism teaches that no religion has finality, while universalism assumes that no person is lost. If these assumptions are accepted, conversion would appear to be a rather banal and unnecessary intrusion on the part of misguided enthusiasts.[28]

William Barclay agrees that identifying conversion with a certain type of religion has given rise to much current confusion. A feeling that conversion is a manifestation of a lower form of religion has made it distasteful to the intellectual. Thus, says Barclay,

> The ideas of conversion and of scholarship have become divorced. It has often been the case that those who were most concerned with conversion have regarded theological colleges as dangerous places, and have even tried to protect their people against the infection which emanates from such places and from those who teach in them.[29]

It is true that the word *conversion* has become associated with hellfire-and-damnation preachers and far-out fanatics who carry their signs on our sidewalks and call down doom on our cities. Because of this confusion some have gone so far as to suggest that the term *conversion* ought to be dropped from the Christian's vocabulary altogether.[30] Nevertheless, as Karl Barth put it, it may be "a term which we cannot avoid despite all its doubtful associations."[31]

Christian conversion cannot be avoided if one does justice to the teachings of the Bible. Since conversion was a basic part of the stuff of Christian history from the very beginning, it would be impossible to understand correctly the New Testament without reference to it. Undeniably, a central place was given to conversion in the first-century church. Bryan Green points this out when he reminds us that the early church was a church of converted men and women. They spoke as converts, they wrote as converts, they exulted as converts.[32] To mute the note of Christian conversion would be to silence the central message of the Bible. "Every single New Testament writing, every gospel and every epistle is concerned with the salvation experienced in and through Jesus."[33] To mute the note of conversion would be to lose the gospel and become blindly disobedient. To mute the note of conversion would be to rob otherwise valid forms of the church's life of their power, if not their very reason for being. As Paul Löffler points out, "Fellowship minus the passion for conversion leads to ghettoism; 'service' minus the call to conversion is a gesture without hope; Christian education minus conversion is religiosity without decision; and 'dialogue' without challenge to conversion remains sterile talk." [34] We cannot be faithful to the biblical record, church history, ourselves, or our local churches without giving Christian conversion a central place.

The place to begin is the Bible. Every attention must be given to that cluster of words in the Bible that helps us understand the mystery and meaning of Christian conversion. As we shall see, Christian conversion is unique, distinctively different from all other forms of conversion.

## QUESTIONS FOR THOUGHT AND DISCUSSION

1. You might try, as the author did, asking a few people how the word *conversion* strikes them and what it means to them. What is your own understanding of the word at this point?

2. What evidence do you see of the quest for religious experience among persons you know? In what various ways is this quest answered?

3. What effect has the current popularization of Christianity through the "media boom" had on your life? Describe both positive and negative results in the faith and life of others.

4. Make a list of the various ways "convert" (verb), "convert" (noun), and "conversion" are used in everyday speech. What is qualitatively different about the Christian meaning of these terms?

# 3. The Biblical Meaning of Conversion

The phenomenon of Babel is perennial. Confusion is nothing new. The church was born in a confusing marketplace of competing religious claims. For the early disciples "confusion of tongues" was the order of the day. Paul's description of Athens confirms this. When he entered Athens he was impressed with the abundance of religions and religious concepts (Acts 17). But isn't Paul's reaction to Athens similar to ours when we read the religious advertisement page in any paper in any major city of the world? At one glance we are struck by a bewildering assortment of religious cults and beliefs. Each has its own code language and each attempts to call people to some sort of conversion.

Because of this confusion a preliminary task in the study of Christian conversion is that of defining terms. Now I am aware that pedantic definitions and etymological distinctions can be wearisome to body and soul. However, clear-cut concepts are indispensable if we wish to talk about Christian conversion at a time of great confusion. As we shall see, Paul Tillich was on target when he observed, "The true nature of conversion is well expressed in the words denoting it in different languages." [1]

The English word *conversion* comes from the Latin *conversus* which is the past participle of *convertere* and basically means "to turn around." It is clear that the *spatial* connotation of "revolving," "reversing," and "changing direction" has been basic to the meaning of the word for many centuries.[2] Moreover, the religious sense of turning to God seems to have been present from the beginning, and the religious use of the word stems from its spatial connotation.[3]

## THE LANGUAGE OF THE BIBLE

When we turn to the Bible, our attempt to define conversion is complicated by the fact that there is no one word in the Old and New Testaments that covers the whole concept. Several words are used, but the Christian understanding of conversion derives mainly from three biblical words: the Old Testament Hebrew word *shûbh*, and the New Testament Greek words *epistrephein* and *metanoein*.

The verb form of *shûbh*, meaning "to return" or "turn back," appears over one thousand times in the Old Testament.[4] *Shûbh* is not merely turning from one thing to another or from one direction to another. Rather, it must be understood in a covenantal context: conversion means "turning back" to God and the covenant previously established between God and Israel. It is to God that the people must return. Old Testament conversion is not an affirmation or reaffirmation of metaphysical beliefs, but a renewed relationship in history involving concrete obedience to God who initiated the covenant in the first place. Therefore, conversion is linked both with the prophetic call to Israel to turn (repent) from its sins and return to God, and with God's readiness to turn towards Israel. The call is to "return" or "turn back" because the relationship between God and Israel is not static but always ongoing.

It is possible to show that the word *conversion* or *repentance* is used in the Old Testament in a morally neutral sense with the meaning of "change one's mind" or "reverse one's former judgment." Nevertheless, the basic meaning of "turning" in the Old Testament involves much more than a mere change of mind, though it includes this. Repentance in the Old Testament represents a reorientation of one's whole life and personality. This involves the adoption of a new ethical line of conduct, a forsaking of sin. This was the fundamental meaning of the call of the prophets when they admonished Israel to "turn again" to God. Tillich affirms this when he says, "the word *shûbh* in Hebrew points to a turning around on one's way, especially in the social and political spheres. It points to a turning away from injustice towards justice, from inhumanity to humanity, from idols to God." [5] The primary emphasis in *shûbh*, therefore, is not on a change of thinking, but rather on a change of directions. It is a change of action, not simply one of ideas. The Old Testament call to repentance is almost always a call to turn back to God, to make a U-turn.

Löffler summarizes a number of consistent characteristics that describe the concept of conversion in the Old Testament: (1) Conversion is participation in a historic movement which requires that people turn again to the God who acts in history. (2) The call to conversion is based on the coming of God and on God's action (which can be an action in the past that is becoming a reality again). Conversion is not just a response to past needs or immediate needs but the ever-new response to God's mighty acts among people. "It is not a human attempt at appeasement but God's offer of a new beginning." (3) Old Testament conversion has a heavy emphasis upon the communal response without excluding the personal dimension. (4) Old Testament conversion involves concrete obedience and a renewed historical relationship to God that is validated by service to one's neighbors.[6]

The new Testament Greek counterparts for *shûbh* are *epistrephein* (and its cognates) and *metanoein*. In these Greek words we find the same basic ideas which are found in *shûbh*. However, since *shûbh* is translated with various Greek compounds in the Septuagint, the Hebrew original is decisive in fixing the meaning of the word.[7] The Septuagint (pre-Christian Greek version of the Old Testament) translates *shûbh* by *epistrephō* or *apostrephō*. The New Testament does not follow the Septuagint but translates *shûbh* as *metanoeō*. This usage has support in other Greek translations of the Hebrew Bible and in Hellenistic Judaism.

The basic meaning of all "conversion" words is that of turning or changing direction. Again, as with *shûbh,* the Greek words imply a turning of the whole human being to God.[8] Now let us look more specifically at the New Testament words for conversion.

In classical or secular Greek *epistrephein* is a common word which denotes movements, turnings, or changes of place, and in this sense it has no technical religious meaning at all. It means "to turn" and is used in both the transitive and the intransitive senses. Thus, it is the common word for the act of causing someone to turn, or of turning one's self. Moreover, as Barclay points out, the word can and often does mean more than physical turning. It can also mean "to turn the mind, the attention to" something else.[9] In the New Testament the verb *epistrephō* occurs thirty-nine times and the noun form appears once. Half of these references are in Luke's writings and about half denote only a physical or spatial movement.[10] When used in ordinary secular contexts its meaning is simply to "turn around," as for example, when Jesus turned around to see who had touched the hem of his garment (Mark 5:30). The word can be used to denote a person's turning to or from anything.

The verb form is often used in the passive voice and is translated "to be converted" (e.g., Acts 3:19, AV) The word can also mean to "return." Although the most popular New Testament verb for "returning" is *hupostrephō* (Luke 2:20, 39), nevertheless, *epistrephō* is sometimes translated "return" (e.g., Matt. 10:13). Thus the word can mean to turn from one direction to another (Mark 5:30, John 21:20), or to return from one place to another (Matt. 12:44), or as Barclay points out, it is frequently used to denote a mental or spiritual turn (Acts 3:19, 9:35).[11] To be sure, when the word is used theologically it carries the basic meaning of *shûbh*. Thus Paul and Luke describe Christians as those who have "turned to God from idols" (1 Thess. 1:9; Acts 14:15).

The Greek verb *metanoeō* ("repent") occurs thirty-two times in the New Testament (e.g., Matt. 3:2; 4:17; 11:20) and the noun form occurs twenty-two times (e.g., Matt. 3:8, Mark 1:4; Luke 3:3). The verb "to change one's mind" appears six times. The literal meaning of *metanoein* "repent" is to "change one's mind." But the New Testament writers were steeped in the Greek translation of the Old Testament (the Septuagint, made several centuries earlier in Egypt). Therefore, if we wish to know what they meant by this word it is necessary to take seriously the Hebrew verb *shûbh*. This enables us to understand that the Greek word *metanoein*, "repent," implies much more than a mere "change of mind." It involves a whole reorientation of the personality, a conversion.

Norman Kraus affirms this: "The primary emphasis in *metanoia* . . . is on reorientation of life—what the Bible calls our 'walk' and what we today refer to as lifestyle." According to Kraus this fundamental reorientation is first a reorientation toward God, the source and ultimate meaning of life, and second it expresses itself as a reorientation of the whole personality in relationship with others. In other words, "*metanoia* is conversion." [12] Hendrikus Berkhof makes the same point. He says, "The Old Testament [and likewise the New Testament] does not have a separate word for 'repentance.' It does contain many terms which carry that notion, and in which it sometimes even dominates. But in that case these words also refer to, for instance, concrete sins or cultic acts or a return to a new obedience." Berkhof observes that while the Hebrew words *shûbh* and the Greek *metanoia* come closest to repentance, "these words are not so much about repentance as about actively breaking with the sinful life, in other words about conversion." He says, "That should warn us against any isolationistic experience of and reflection on repentance. The Bible does not even have a term for repentance without conversion." [13]

Hans Küng gives his support to this interpretation by translating *metanoia* as "conversion." He claims that it has been misleading to render the word as "repentance." For *metanoia*, like "conversion," means a fundamental and total reorientation of one's life towards God. "It is a decisive change of will, an awareness changed from the roots upward, a new basic attitude, a different scale of values." [14]

What is common to all these words, both in their general cultural usage and in their transfer to a religious context is the theme of *turning*. Moreover, these words and the images they provoke suggest two elements: the negation of a preceding thought and action and the affirmation of a new direction.

This helps us to see that there is a two-fold direction implicit in the Christian concept of conversion. For this reason Barclay claims that conversion involves a *terminus-a-quo* and a *terminus-ad-quem*, that is, a turning from something and a turning towards something.[15] This two-fold direction can be seen in Paul's statement to Agrippa. The apostle quotes from the commission given him by Jesus: "I send you to open their eyes and turn them from darkness to light, from the dominion of Satan to God" (Acts 26:18). The essence of conversion is a turn towards God which includes a turning away from idols (1 Thess. 1:9), from darkness and the power of Satan (Acts 26:18), and from evil.

Moreover, to show the linkages between *epistrephō* and *metanoeō* the two words sometimes appear in the same passage of scripture. It is in this way that Luke links inward and outward turning. In Luke 17:4 we read: "If your brother wrongs you, rebuke him; and if he repents, forgive him. Even if he wrongs you seven times in a day and comes back [turns again] to you seven times saying, I repent, you are to forgive him" (Luke 17:4). In addition, *epistrephō* and *metanoeō* occur together twice in the book of Acts. In Acts 3:19 Peter says, "Repent then and turn to God." In the story of Acts 26:18-20 Paul tells Agrippa that he "sounded the call to repent and turn to God, and to prove their repentance by good works."

Charles Edwin Carlston is very convincing in his study of the two-fold direction of conversion. He says, "If any distinction is to be made between *metanoein* and *epistrephein* in the New Testament, it is that *metanoein* emphasizes somewhat more strongly the new element of turning away from the old, *epistrephein* turning toward the new" (e.g., Acts 3:10; 26:20).[16]

## MEANINGS IN THE BIBLE

Thus far in our study we have seen how the word *conversion*, derived as it is from the language of everyday experience, is a word covering a wide range of emotions, relationships, changes in attitudes, direction, lifestyle, and affiliations. Moreover, we have observed that conversion is a psychological phenomenon common to many religions. We have seen that changes of allegiance, direction, and lifestyle as well as psychological releases can happen quite apart from Christian conversion. In this sense conversion is not just a Christian word.

Realizing this confusion and knowing that the current usage of the word cannot be the ultimate authority in our understanding of Christian conversion, we have turned to the biblical text to trace its meaning in the Old Testament and how that meaning was transferred to the New Testament. From our biblical studies we can delineate the following ways in which biblical conversion is distinctive and unique. From the Old Testament perspective we learn that:

1. Biblical conversion signifies a turning from sin and a turning to God. As Erik Routley insists, the word *conversion*, in both the original Hebrew and Greek, means "a decisive turning—stopping in your tracks, attending to an order, and then turning and making for the new destination." [17]

2. Biblical conversion is more than remorse or regret for our sins. It is more than a change of mind and more than an affirmation of beliefs, though it includes all of these. Biblical conversion is a fundamental reorientation of the whole person, a reorientation which requires concrete obedience. It is the total turning of the total person towards the God who acts in history to redeem.

3. This reorientation is both personal and communal, and not one without the other. The personal and social sides of turning to God must be held together. Each person is called to respond to God's action in history, but this personal turning issues forth in a reorientation of the whole personality in relationship with others.

4. Biblical conversion is not viewed as a single act but a life-long process, a participation in a historic movement. It has a past, present, and future focus. We not only turn to God's action in the past and affirm it again and again, but we also orient ourselves towards God's action in the present and future. To be sure, biblical conversion has its beginnings, but by its nature it necessitates many turns all along one's pilgrimage.

5. From beginning to end biblical conversion is response to the initiative of God. It is an act of the human being which is possible only because of a previous act of God.

From the New Testament perspective we learn that Christian

conversion, by its very nature, relates to Christ and the kingdom of God. "Jesus is Christ" is the central message of the New Testament. This is the message that holds the twenty-seven books of the New Testament together and it is the thread of unity which runs through twenty centuries of Christian history.[18] Therefore, the urgency for Christian conversion does not derive from the peculiar psychological make-up of an individual or from the person's need to make a particular decision or to have a particular kind of experience. The New Testament basis for repentance (conversion) is christological. Its focus is Jesus who is the Christ.

This same Jesus called for conversion in the light of the dawning kingdom of God. Prior to Jesus, John the Baptist had added a new dimension to the Old Testament prophetic preaching of repentance by focusing upon the imminent coming of the kingdom and a water baptism granting the forgiveness of sins. "Bear fruit that befits repentance," he said. "Every tree that does not bear fruit is cut down and thrown into the fire" (Matt. 3:8,10, KJV). John the Baptist and the Old Testament prophets knew that in authentic repentance God takes the initiative and gives a person a new heart and a new spirit. They knew that repentance in the deepest sense of the word is beyond human power. So they looked forward to the time when God would accomplish this. In Jesus' preaching of the kingdom of God he was saying that the time "has come." He said, "The time has come; the kingdom of God is upon you; repent, and believe the gospel" (Mark 1:15).

Therefore, because of God's revelation in Jesus Christ, conversion is more than a demand; it has become a possibility. What we could not do for ourselves, God has accomplished (Mark 10:27). Response to the preaching of the kingdom is something joyful and new. It brings radical change and renewal. The joy of the kingdom is beyond all measure, and when it seizes us it penetrates our inmost being. Therefore, all other things pale into insignificance compared with the surpassing worth of the kingdom of God. The impact of the joyful news of the kingdom is so overpowering it fills the heart with gladness and makes life's whole aim the willingness to follow Jesus in unreserved surrender. So, the governing principle of the converted life is that it is lived out under the lordship of Christ and the kingdom. Christ's authority over us is so total that it leads inevitably to a total reappraisal of every aspect of life and a radical reorientation in terms of our world-view, our behavior, and all our relationships.

Conversion as a process is connected with the kingdom of God. This kingdom is a new order of life which God offers in Jesus Christ through the enabling power of the Holy Spirit. "It is a future reality which is, nevertheless, anticipated in the present. It is a reality that we experience both personally and in the community of faith. It is a reflex of what God has done, is doing, and will do, but it is basically discernible in the obedience of faith. Christian conversion revolves around this future-present, socio-personal, reflection-action reality." [19]

Since the dawning of the kingdom through Christ's advent is the primary context of conversion in the New Testament, we can, according to Paul Löffler, derive from this fact three decisive criteria for Christian conversion:

1. It reinforces that the triune God is the author of every aspect of conversion. The givenness of the kingdom means that its reality is there before persons acknowledge it by conversion and that all human beings live within the "gravitational field" of that reality.

2. The universal significance of the kingdom means that the call to conversion is now explicitly linked with the commission to preach 'to all nations' (Luke 24:47; Acts 2:38). Just as the prophets expound Israel's destiny within that of the nations, so conversion is concerned with the destiny of all human beings . . . .

3. The kingdom represents a reality which is moving towards the future and the end of time. It leads to the restoration of the whole cosmos, to the renewal of all things. With it conversion shares that eschatological character. It is not an end in itself but the beginning of a recreation that must ultimately comprise *ta panta* (all peoples)." [20]

Since the message of the New Testament is the announcement that the kingdom of God has come in Christ, this signals the fact that the day of repentance-conversion has begun (Luke 1:16; Matt. 3:12). Thus, Jesus heralds the dawning kingdom by calling people to "turn" and "trust." Repentance and faith are the necessary responses to Jesus and his message of the kingdom. Through repentance and faith the saving initiative of God is translated into human experience. In making repentance and faith the keynote of his kingdom preaching (Mark 1:15), Jesus indicated the integral connection between the two. They are two sides of the same coin, for without trusting the divine revelation in Christ there can be no genuine "turning." Thus repentance and faith are interrelated. Conversion is made possible by faith that the time of salvation is fulfilled and the reign of God at hand. Conversely, radical trust (faith) is possible only through repentance which recognizes personal guilt and the need for grace.

Therefore, forgiveness is inseparable from repentance. Without repentance forgiveness turns into an attempt to excuse ourselves. Judaism taught that God forgives a repentant sinner. But the question arises, "Who can repent? Can I change a bad relationship with God by simply deciding to? Is the matter that simple? Is the matter in my hands? Not at all, because God is not an object to be manipulated, but a personal reality. Moreover, repentance and faith belong together because both repentance and faith are not prior events but an extended act.

Faith, too, is a form of turning. Trusting God is itself an act of turning from other gods and other allegiances. Thus, faith is not believing that an idea is true, but fundamental trust in God that undergirds all our allegiances. It follows that what we do and how we do it manifests our faith. Therefore, repentance and faith are not just a matter of soul or body. They involve the total self and the total life. Since this is true, it is possible to speak of a *life* of repentance and faith. Repentance and faith mean Godward turning with one's entire life. They constitute an effort to orient life towards the grace of God, and are a resolute loyalty to the one God who is the center of life.

Suffice it to say, Christian conversion is conversion to Christ and the kingdom, and this means to bring one's total life and culture under the authority of the living God and into conformity with God's kingdom. As Gabriel Fackre rightly observes, "Christian conversion is a radically and totally new posture, the changing of one's feet, relationships, and behavior as well as one's mind and heart." Christian conversion is more than just the changing of labels, denominations, or religions. It is rather the drastic about-face of a new creature which leads us to "keep company with the suffering of God in the world. Conversion marks Christianity, therefore, as a demanding moral religion whose entry point requires a decisive turn, a rigorous internal and external reorientation." [21]

## QUESTIONS FOR THOUGHT AND DISCUSSION

1. The author shows that the three biblical words that are translated "conversion" all suggest a "turning" from one thing to another. Make two lists, "Turning from . . . " and "Turning to . . . ," that describe your own experience of conversion.

2. The Old Testament concept of conversion is summarized in four affirmations (p. 33). Try putting these into your own words, and then use them to examine your own experience.

3. The author notes that repentance and faith are interrelated in Jesus' kingdom preaching, "two sides of the same coin" (p. 40). Describe the relationship between repentance and faith as you have experienced it.

# 4. Conversion Is God's Idea

From our study of the biblical meaning of conversion we learned that God is the originator and initiator, the source and goal of Christian conversion. Since God is central to the act and process, Christian conversion must be viewed in theological perspective. (If the action of God is central, how could it be otherwise?) In viewing Christian conversion in theological perspective I shall first attempt to show how Christian conversion derives from the nature of God, i.e., how it is possible because of who God is. Second, I shall draw out some implications that are crucial to our study.

It must be admitted that who God is (God's nature) and what God does (God's action) cut right across our theories and formulas. In many ways our anthropomorphisms are not worthy of God, who is beyond all our descriptions. The human cannot comprehend the fullness of God's nature. God's nature can only be hinted at by our frail formulas, analogies, and figures of speech. However, having acknowledged this limitation, we can learn from the scriptures many dynamic truths about God. The numerous analogies of the Bible leave us with little doubt but that God is a living, envisioning, willing, acting Spirit—a personal God (Exod. 3:14; Eph. 1:9-11). Our reserve about personal metaphors and analogies used in connection with God should not cause us to deny the personal element in God. Theologically, these metaphors serve to signify that "while at least personal, God is inexhaustably more so. God is not less than our own self-directing, purposive, free, choosing selves." [1]

If God is not in some sense personal, if God is only the "Wholly

Other," then as a living person I can only conclude that God has nothing more to do with me, nor I with God. But such a view of God would contradict the whole history of salvation out of which the Jewish and Christian faiths have arisen. Such a view would ignore the history of our origins. Through the history of salvation (*Heilsgeschichte*) God has always been in search of lost humans. God seeks us "down the corridors of time" and is revealed in history. The living God has meaning in the context of history and in dialogue with persons. Karl Barth affirms this by saying, "who God is, and what He is in his deity, that He demonstrates and reveals not in the empty space of a divine isolation, but rather authentically just where He exists, speaks, and acts as the partner of man (though he is certainly absolutely superior)." [2]

Jürgen Moltmann presses this point further by saying:

> Between the Trinity in its origins before time and the eschatological glorifying and unifying of God lies the whole history of God's dealings with the world. By opening himself for this history and entering into it in his seeking love, . . . God also experiences this history of the world in its breadth and depth. We must drop the philosophical axioms about the nature of God. God is not unchangeable, if to be unchangeable means that he could not in the freedom of his love open himself to the changeable history of his creation. God is not incapable of suffering, if this means that in the freedom of his love he would not be receptive to suffering over the contradictions of man and the self-destruction of his creation. God is not invulnerable, if this means that he could not open himself to the pain of the cross.[3]

The living God spoken of in scriptures is therefore not the God of the philosophers outside time and space, a kind of motionless essence. The living God is not passive but active. Moreover, the living God is not the sum and substance of the most sublime conceptions of the mind. How can a person be expected to love and be loyal to or enter into a creative relationship with an abstraction? The living God is personal, One whose heart feels and longs and loves, One whose voice speaks. The living God is One who intervenes, who acts, who seeks and sends, who suffers, who enters history in Jesus Christ and enters into human beings by the Holy Spirit. The living God comes into the broken order of our lives to live with us in Person-to-person relationship. Christian conversion, then, is born of the fact that God is a missionary God who moves out to people and wants people to experience conversion. Our God is a seeking God.

## THE GOD WHO SEEKS

In many ways the Bible is a book about the initiative of God. It teaches us that we can never take God by surprise. God always makes the first move. God is always "in the beginning." Therefore, the scriptures do not so much emphasize our groping after God as they do God's seeking after us. Now it is undeniably true that people seek God, and they should. Some people tend to speak of their conversion as "finding God," but this is mistaken on two counts. First, it tends to imply that God has been lost or misplaced and, second, it tends to put too much emphasis upon human activity and too little upon divine initiative. People cannot "find God," simply because God has never been lost!

It is impossible to predate the initiative of God, because the living God seeks us long before our seeking begins. This point is beautifully illustrated in the conversion of Blaise Pascal. No doubt Pascal's vigorous search for meaning helped to prepare him for his conversion experience of 1654. But, as Brian Mahan observes, "It seems inadequate to describe Pascal's reaction as merely the ecstasy of discovery. The events seem more direct: Pascal seems to have felt, after his long search for meaning, meaning suddenly had sought him out and addressed him. His language is more the language of encounter than the language of discovery." [4] The language of encounter is more appropriate in talking about Christian conversion because it puts emphasis upon God's action as Seeker. This is what the anonymous poet had in mind when he wrote:

I sought the Lord, and afterward I knew
He moved my soul to seek him, seeking me;
It was not I that found, O Savior true;
No, I was found of thee.

Thou didst reach forth thy hand and mine enfold;
I walked and sank not on the storm-vexed sea;
'Twas not so much that I on thee took hold
As thou, dear Lord, on me.

I find, I walk, I love, but oh, the whole
Of love is but my answer, Lord, to thee!
For thou wert long beforehand with my soul;
Always thou lovedst me.[5]

## THE GOD WHO SENDS

Not only is God's initiative and action illustrated in God's seeking, it can also be seen in God's action as Sender. This emphasis is caught up in the important New Testament word, *mission*. The word *mission* comes from the Latin *missio* which is a translation of two Greek words, *pempo* and *apostello*. All of these words have to do with sending. If you break the word *mission* down into its constituent parts it reveals four truths. There is someone who sends: God. There is that which God sends: the message, which is actually a self-revealing communication. There is the messenger, and there is the recipient. As you can see, from beginning to end, this is a Person-to-person concept. A Person on one end is reaching out to persons on the other end of the line. This is just another way of saying that mission (and conversion) begins in God. It is a part of God's nature and will.

The theme of God's action as Sender winds like an unbroken thread through the biblical text. God sent a Babylonian shepherd prince named Abraham from the famous city of Haran into the great unknown promising to bless him and the world through him. God sent Joseph into Egypt in order to preserve a remnant of the faithful. God sent Moses, stammering into the presence of Pharaoh in order to lead Abraham's oppressed descendants out of Egyptian slavery. God entered into a covenant relationship with these people in order to make of them a representative people, a holy nation, a kingdom of priests (Exod. 19:5-6). When Israel turned to disobedience and idolatry, allowed the development of gaping disparities between the affluent and the poor, turned from God and sought security in foreign alliances and treaties, God sent forth a succession of prophets with words of warning and promise.

"But when the right time finally came, God sent his own Son. He came as the son of a humble mother and lived under the Jewish law to set free those who were under the law, so that we might become God's children" (Gal. 4:4-5, TEV). During his short ministry, Jesus sent forth first the apostles and then the seventy as an extension of his own preaching, teaching, and healing ministry. After his death, resurrection, and ascension, Christ widened the scope of the mission by sending forth the Spirit on the day of Pentecost. Now the Son sends as he himself was sent, and his mission includes all who call him Lord (John 20:20-21).

Jürgen Moltmann insists that Jesus' history must be understood as the revelation of the living nature of God. The Gospels present the history of Jesus in the light of his sending—his mission. He is sent from God into the world for the purpose of salvation. "The word 'sending' is intended to comprehend the perception of the whole appearance, history and meaning of Christ in the light of God." According to Moltmann, the mission of Jesus was certainly not a chance historical development, but rather it finds "its foundation in God himself. . . . As God appears in history as the sending Father and the sent Son so he must earlier have been in himself." Therefore, in the messianic mission of Jesus we confront the revelation of the living nature of God. If this were not the case the experience of the Spirit and fellowship with Jesus could not be understood as experience and fellowship with God. But, as Moltmann concludes, "It is clear that in the sending of the Son and in the sending of the Spirit, men have to do with God himself." In the sending of Jesus Christ and the Spirit we witness the climax of God's seeking love.[6]

Thus we can see that the possibility of Christian conversion comes as the result of God's activity and has its origin in the very nature of our triune God. God the Father shows his mission through his sending activity to humankind and by his perpetual working in creation. God the Son is the climactic expression of God's sending activity toward persons. Through him a relationship with God is made available to all persons. God the Holy Spirit empowers the church and sends it forth into mission. Moltmann concludes: "A Christian doctrine of the Trinity which is bound to the history of Christ and the history of the Spirit must conceive the Trinity as the Trinity of the sending and seeking love of God which is opened from its very origin. The triune God is the God who is open to man, open to the world, and open to time." [7]

## THE GOD WHO LOVES

God the Creator, Seeker, and Sender is also the God of love. With indefatigable and never-failing love God seeks us out. The realization that we are supported, surrounded, and sought by a final reality which we call "love" is the most amazing, incomprehensible, and marvelous fact of human existence. Upon this reality our understanding of Christian conversion will either stand or fall, because any attempt to understand conversion in theological perspective will be an elaboration of this wonderful reality. Since love is the essential characteristic of the nature of God (1 John 4:8-16) and all Christian love is derivative of God's love, the heart of Christian conversion is the fact that the living God manifests himself as Love. God loves us long before we love God and it is because we know God loves that we turn our lives Godward. God's invitation to repentance and belief is a pledge to accept us. But what is the nature of this love that will not let us go, this love that meets us before we turn? What does love mean?

The current uses of the word *love* are of little help in probing the depth of the Christian affirmation, "God is love." Like all words, the word *love* is derived from the language of human experience. It is used to cover a wide range of emotions and relationships, from the crassest form of greed to the most sublime form of self-sacrifice. We use it in a variety of different contexts, and it means different things to different people. We say, "I love apple pie," or, "I love my cat," or, "I love my great little car," or, "I love my wife," or, "I love my husband," or, "I love God." Now it is perfectly obvious that we do not mean the same thing when we say, "I love apple pie," as when we say, "I love God."

Love *as such* is not divine in character. Therefore, it is not possible to understand the love of God by simply extending what the word *love* means to us. This points up the mistake in saying that "love is God." This statement imposes an improper order, for it starts with our human experience of love and then presumes to say that God's love is like ours. But compared even with the highest form of human love, God's love is unique. Karl Barth says, "God's loving is a divine being and action distinct from every loving in the fact that it is holy. As holy, it is characterized by the fact that God, as He seeks and creates fellowship, is always the Lord. He therefore distinguishes and maintains His own will as against every other will." [8] The living God is the subject who determines the nature and content of love. Our concept of love does not determine the nature of God, but the nature of God determines what love is. God is the subject and love is the predicate. It is important not to confuse these realities or to treat them as if they were interchangeable.

Human love is always mixed with ambiguous motives. But God loves us and moves in our direction before we have made any move towards God. First John 4:19 says, "We love because he first loved us." This means that our ability to experience and to give love comes through God's prior love for us. It also means that God's love cannot be earned, compelled, or forced. As human beings we cannot force the divine love to enter our lives. Paul Tillich concludes, "The attempt to do so belongs directly to the ambiguity of religion and indirectly to the ambiguity of culture and morality. If religious devotion, moral obedience, or scientific honesty could compel the divine Spirit to 'descend' to us, the spirit which 'descended' would be the human spirit in a religious disguise. It would be, and often is, simply man's spirit ascending, the natural form of man's self transcendence. The finite cannot force the infinite; men cannot compel God." [9] Only the action of God wherein God is manifested as the one who loves can tell us what it means to say "God is love." Only God can reveal God, and only Love can reveal love.

The scriptures speak eloquently of God's self-giving love to humanity in a covenant with Israel and in the life of Jesus Christ. In the first place the scriptures teach us that, in keeping with God's nature, God's love is personal. Love's motive and origin can only be found in the innermost personal being of God. Divine love is a part of the mystery of God's personality, and as a result, God's love is often connected with a daring use of anthropomorphic expressions (e.g., Hosea 11:8, Jer. 31:30, Isa. 63:15).[10] In the Old Testament God's love is sometimes compared with the love of a father or a mother (Isa. 49:15; 66:13). At other times the love of God is compared with that of a husband or a friend (Hosea; Isa. 41:8). However, it is always clear that God's love is only *comparable* to human love and goes far beyond these forms of love. God's love is infinitely more than what we call love in human relationships.

Next, the scriptures teach us that God's love is unmotivated and spontaneous. This can be observed first of all in the fact that God's love is not caused by the attractiveness or worth of its object. For example, the cause of God's love for Israel did not lie in any inherent qualities that Israel possessed, but rather in the personal being of God. Thus, when we look at those whom God loves we can find no explanation in them for such love. God told Israel, "It was not because you are more in number than any other people that the Lord set his love upon you and chose you" (Deut. 7:7). It was not because Israel was lovable that God loved Israel. The only explanation given for God's love was "The Lord loves you because the Lord loves you" (v. 8). God's love has no cause prior to itself. Therefore, God goes on loving despite the fact that Israel turns aside and becomes a stiff-necked people. Justice and reason would have demanded Israel's destruction, but God refuses to destroy her (Hosea 11:9). The ground for this refusal was in God's divine being: "For I am God, and not a man, the holy one in your midst" (Hosea 11:9; Isa. 55:7f).

The unmotivated, spontaneous nature of God's love can also be seen in the fact that God's love is full and free. God does not have to love us. When the living God acts in love, these acts are free. It is not because God needs us for the purpose of self-fulfillment that we are loved. Our own pride might cause us to think that we are needed as an antidote for God's loneliness and boredom, but this is a distortion of the biblical portrait of God.

This emphasis upon God's love, initiative, action, or self-revelation implies that God must be a communicative God. This puts us in touch with the amazing realization that God is the one who is self-giving, the one whose aim is to make people's lives meaningful and full by allowing them to share in the richness of God's own being. God's nature is self-giving Love. When and if these words are really *heard*, their message fills the heart with amazement and awe. God's self-giving love is an awesome mystery, strange and incomparable. What a pity that we often miss the wonder of God's love. All of our lives we have heard, "God is love." But we greet these words by saying, "Of course, so what else is new?" We have heard the statement so often that we take it for granted, and it evokes in us about as much surprise and wonder as the arrival of the evening paper. Our sensibilities seem blunted to the realization that God's love is always a miracle and always the last thing we deserve. Our human pride causes us to forget that the source and reason for God's love are in God, not in us. It is impossible to account for God's love by way of any outside stimuli.

Though it is simplistic to draw a sharp contrast between the Old and New Testament portrayals of the love of God, it is evident that in Christ God's love receives a more radical and universal expression. In a recent book, Hans Küng makes this bold statement of faith: "The God of the New Testament has a name and a face. He is the God of Israel, who is also the Father of Jesus Christ. The God of the New Testament reveals Himself not only in the history of the nation but in an individual human form in which God's Son, Word, will and love assumed flesh." [11] Therefore, in order to witness God's love in its fullness and in order to discover how God's love makes Christian conversion possible, we must now turn to the New Testament understanding of love.

We have said that in the Bible, love is the essential characteristic of the divine nature (1 John 4:8-16) from which all genuine love is derived (4:19). However, all that the New Testament has to say about God's love can be summed up in the two words: "Jesus Christ." In Jesus Christ the revelation of God's love reached its zenith. Again, Hans Küng says, "The Christian feature of the Christian God is this Christ Himself, through whom believers know this God, the one God of the fathers through whom this God reveals Himself for believers. ... The ultimate distinguishing feature of Christianity as a whole—according to Paul—is quite literally 'Jesus as the crucified Christ.' " [12]

What we can finally know of God's love for humanity we know through God's self-revelation in Jesus Christ (Rom. 8:39). According to the New Testament, Jesus reveals the divine love by what he says, does, and is. It is through God's action in Jesus Christ that we know what love is (1 John 3:16). Jesus is the exponent of God's love in action (Luke 15), and he is the exemplar who, by his deeds of compassion, reveals divine love again and again (Luke 7:34). Not only did Jesus' love reach out to the old, the poor, the weak, and the despised; his love reached out to the rich young ruler. And, as we shall see, he allowed himself to be cursed, laughed at, ignored, slapped in the face, spit upon, stripped naked, and nailed up to die as God's own proof of love (Rom. 5:8). His words to Zacchaeus are informing, "For the Son of Man has come to seek and to save that which was lost" (Luke 19:10). Jesus is the one through whom God reconciles the world to himself (2 Corinthians 5:19). He is the one who gives substance to the word *love*.

In the final analysis the word *love* cannot fully describe God or Jesus. For the Christian it is Jesus Christ who gives meaning to the words *God* and *love*. Jesus Christ discloses God's love (John 3:16). Thus, God's love has its ultimate historical reference in Jesus Christ, and since God's love has such a concrete, historical reference, it is not just a matter of mythical or ethical ideals. It is a substantial and real love available to all.

In Jesus' life, death, and resurrection, God is revealed as unconditional love, *agape*. *Agape* is the important New Testament word for a love that is central to the Christian faith; a love which is the unmerited, spontaneous, uncalculated compassion of God's own heart. It is this love that meets us explicitly or implicitly on practically every page of the Gospels. In keeping with God's self-revelation in the Old Testament, *agape* is a distinct love which goes out to human beings for no other reason than because they are persons, and not because they are agreeable or attractive or lovable.

Paul Tillich outlines three fundamental qualities of *agape*. The first quality is the acceptance of the object of love without restrictions. The second is love's determination to hold fast to this acceptance in spite of the estranged state of its object. The third quality is the hope and expectation of the re-establishment of the holiness and dignity of love's object through love's acceptance.[13] This teaches us that *agape* is a stubborn and empowering love which persists in an unswerving pursuit of its object. But, in addition to Tillich's observations, it must be noted that *agape* is also an open love which leaves the object the "maneuvering room of freedom."[14]

Human beings always encounter *agape* in the form of a gift from God, a gift which they can accept or reject. This is best understood in the familiar verse, John 3:16: "God loved the world so much that he *gave*. . . . " There is no way to earn or merit this love. We usually experience God's love through the self-giving love of others; nevertheless, if we experience it at all we experience it as a gift. This being the case, we have no claim on *agape*. Because this love has been poured out as a gift, our only legitimate response is one of grateful discipleship.

In summary, we have said that God has created us and loves us. God's missionary outreach moves out to us and calls us to repentance. God is in no way dependent upon us, yet chooses to be in relationship with us. God's initiative and action are illustrated in a seeking, sending love. God's love is supremely disclosed in Jesus Christ. In Jesus' life, death, and resurrection, God is revealed as unconditional love, *agape*. Now, what does all of this imply with regard to our understanding of Christian conversion?

## IMPLICATIONS FOR CHRISTIAN CONVERSION

First and foremost, Christian conversion is, in part, a response to one's realization of what God is really like. Thus some understanding of the nature of the living God is necessary in order for Christian conversion to happen. The late William Barclay shares the following insightful observation:

> If God is no more than indifferent, there is no point in turning to one who in any event does not care. . . . There is no point in turning to a God who by His very nature would not even notice if you turned. If God is simply inexorable law, avenging justice, unapproachable holiness, then there is no point in turning to Him. There would be no welcome there; there would be nothing but condemnation and obliteration. . . . We cannot turn to God unless we know that God is love.[15]

John Wesley was well aware of this truth and, therefore, put primary emphasis upon the love of God. He wanted the Methodist movement to be worthy of the God who brought it into being. He looked on every side and saw either people of "no religion at all or men of a lifeless, formal religion." He believed that there was "a better religion to be attained. . . ." He said, "This we conceive to be no other than love: the love of God and of all mankind. . . . This love we believe to be the medicine of life, the never-failing remedy for all the evils of a disordered world, for all the misery and vices of men."[16] Again, he said, "Love existed from eternity in God, the great ocean of love. . . . Love is the end of all the commandments of God. Love is the end, the sole end, of every dispensation of God, from the beginning of the world to the consummation of all things. And it will endure when heaven and earth flee away; for 'love' alone 'never faileth' (1 Cor. 13:8)."[17] Because of this deep conviction regarding the love of God, Wesley felt it necessary to begin his preaching in a new place with "a general declaration of the love of God to sinners and His willingness that they should be saved."[18]

The way one's understanding of the nature of God impacts Christian conversion can also be seen in Martin Luther's experience:

I greatly longed to understand Paul's epistle to the Romans and nothing stood in my way but that one expression, "the justice [righteousness] of God," because I took it to mean that justice whereby God is just and deals justly in punishing the unjust. My situation was that, although an impeccable monk, I stood before God as a sinner troubled in conscience and I had no confidence that my merit would assuage Him. Therefore, I did not love a just and angry God, but rather hated and murmured against Him. Yet I clung to the dear Paul and had a great yearning to know what he meant.

Night and day I pondered until I saw the connection between the justice of God and the statement that the "just shall live by his faith." Then I grasped that the justice of God is that righteousness by which through grace and sheer mercy God justifies us through faith. Thereupon, I felt myself to be reborn and to have gone through open doors into paradise. The whole of scripture took on a new meaning. And whereas before "justice of God" had filled me with hate, now it became to me inexpressibly sweet in greater love.[19]

Basic to Christian conversion is the realization that God is love. We will not turn to God in faith unless we know that God is love.

Second, the fact that God's seeking love reaches out to us through the history of patriarchs and prophets and ultimately through the person of Jesus Christ is ample proof that God "speaks to persons through persons seeking to accomplish His purposes." [20] We encounter God's love through persons, and our love for persons follows from our love for God. This, of course, affirms the personal nature of God and says that it is impossible for us to exist apart from this world of the personal. H. H. Farmer concludes that God made humanity in accordance with this purpose, therefore, God never enters into relationship with a person apart from other human beings. "The individual is related all the time to his neighbor in God and to God in his neighbor, even when he is not aware of it, even when he denies it, and in that relationship, his distinctive quality as a human person resides." [21] This point has tremendous implications not only for our understanding of Christian conversion but our understanding of evangelism as well. We will consider these in greater detail in the following chapters.

Third, to say that God is the originator of Christian conversion implies that conversion is God's idea and not the church's invention. The derivation of Christian conversion is not an ecclesiological phenomenon. It is a theological one. God has not given the church the luxury of debating whether or not Christian conversion is necessary, as if conversion were the church's idea. The church is not the end for which conversion is the means. No, Christian conversion is the end for which the church is the means.

Certainly John Wesley's ministry exemplified this point. He was willing, against the most severe ecclesiological pressure, to move his pulpit into the open air in order to communicate the gospel of God's saving grace. His continued emphasis upon the sacrament as a "converting ordinance" and his dauntless emphasis on the gospel call to repentance and the promise of pardon are ample proof that Christian conversion was the primary focus of his powerful ministry. Wesley's most often used preaching texts were Mark 1:15 (190 times) and Isaiah 55:6 or 7 (202 times). His primary preaching theme was "repent and accept God's grace in Christ." [22] For Wesley, the church existed as a means to communicate this message.

Fourth, we have seen that Christian conversion happens on God's terms and at God's initiative and in accordance with God's love. Initially, Christian conversion does not depend on anything that a person can do or be, but rather, on what God has done and continues to be. This implies that Christian conversion cannot be demanded, commanded, or deserved. It is a matter of God's gracious activity and not a matter of human gumption, glands, or goodness.[23]

John Wesley understood this very well. He knew that from their own lives people cannot discover the truth about God. He recognized that it was the prerogative of God to break up the fallow ground of the soul, and implant the seed of new life. Over and over he placed emphasis upon divine initiative. He looked to God alone to bring about conversions.[24] Wesley knew that Christian conversion was not within humanity's natural capacity to initiate. As Albert Outler points out, "It is not, at bottom, part of the human potential, . . . It is God's initiative that makes possible our response; it is his self-presentation in Christ that frees us to accept his acceptance of us."[25]

Fifth, it is necessary to see God as both the originator and initiator of Christian conversion in order to offset the impression that conversion is a human achievement. This is precisely the impression given when the church allows itself to slip into the outlook of the world and supposes that the key to evangelistic success is business efficiency, and that converts come automatically if we will only follow the instructions given in our "Do It Yourself" manuals. But one does not experience Christian conversion by "whipping up the will—by striving a little harder, by being a little more faithful in religious exercises, by being more regular in church attendance, by lifting yourself by your bootstraps. . . . You don't find God through climbing a ladder of self-effort rung by rung to find Him on the topmost rung of the ladder of worthiness. This is an egocentric attempt at salvation."[26] The living God is encountered at the bottom-most rung of the ladder, for God comes down the ladder of incarnation and meets us where we are as sinners.[27]

Again, John Wesley's experience highlights the folly of our own doomed and frenzied attempts at self-salvation. As Robert Tuttle points out, "Wesley, in 1725, made religion the business of his life. He wanted to clean himself up that God might love him."[28] Wesley said, "I began to alter the whole form of my conversation, and to set in earnest upon 'a new life.' I set apart an hour or two a day for religious retirement. I communicated every week. I worked against all sin, whether in word or deed. I began to aim at, and pray for, inward holiness. So that now, doing so much and living so good a life, I doubted not but I was a good Christian."[29] Later (1738), when he resolved to seek a living faith, Wesley said, "I found it necessary to renounce all dependence, in whole or in part, upon my own works or righteousness—on which I had really grounded my hope of salvation, though I knew it not, from my youth up." [30] Wesley began to realize that only the divine initiative was capable of establishing a basis for reconciliation between God and rebellious humanity. God's work in Christ eliminates all efforts towards self-salvation, for it declares that the new basis for relationship is God's love and God's love alone.

Thus it is clear that the only way in which we can be brought to Christian conversion is for God to act. In order for the person to "turn around," an intervention from God is necessary. Without this intervention conversion is impossible. The primordial element of conversion, therefore, is not a human effort toward self-salvation; it is, rather, an encounter with the living God. It is God who makes possible Christian conversion. God imparts the Holy Presence to us. This is the constitutive part of conversion. But how does this happen? Next we shall see how God makes conversion possible by being accessible to us.

## QUESTIONS FOR THOUGHT AND DISCUSSION

1. The author says, "The living God seeks us long before our seeking begins" (p. 44). Take some time to reflect on your life, and identify ways God has taken the initiative in seeking you. Through what persons? Through what ministries of the church? Through what other experiences?

2. God is also a Sender. What persons—both historical and contemporary—has God sent whose mission has had an impact on your Christian development? To whom is God now sending you?

3. God also takes the initiative in love—love that is prior, personal, spontaneous, full, free, unearned, unconditional, and unending. You might write a paragraph on the love of God as you have experienced it, without using the word *love* at all.

4. Try putting the author's five implications for Christian conversion (pp. 53-57) into your own words.

# 5. The Good News of Salvation

Earlier it was noted that God is a communicative God. It follows that "Christianity is a religion of communication." You ask, "But is this not true of other religions?" And I answer, "Yes, but it is the nature and content of the communication that makes Christianity distinctive. Christian communication is not special information about things divine. It is not laws or mystical insights arrived at by intensive introspection and meditation. It is not a bit of knowledge passed from one person to another for his or her enlightenment. It is not a divine spark we each could find for ourselves within ourselves.

No, the "Word" of communication that makes Christianity distinctive is a Word-Event, an event in which God takes the initiative and is known to humanity through a particular person, Jesus of Nazareth.[1] According to our faith, an extraordinary event which came at the peak of a lengthy process of revelation has changed and is changing the whole context of human living, the event of God in the birth, life, death, and resurrection of Jesus Christ. It is this Christ-Event which sets Christian conversion in motion.[2] It is the message of God's suffering, redeeming, reconciling love in Christ that initiates a new life in Christ within the Body of Christ, the church.

As you can see, this communication is more than an affirmation of ideals which people must practice. It is more than an explanation of life and its problems about which people may argue. It is rather the announcement of an Event with which people must reckon.[3] Of its very nature the Event-content of Christian communication demands a reckoning.

Christian communication is proclamation in the fullest sense. It is an announcement that summons and compels us to reply. Christian communication involving the calling, justification, and liberation of human beings comes from this Event. As the Apostle Paul makes clear, we are justified by faith; we are in Christ Jesus by God's own act, for God has made Christ Jesus our wisdom and our righteousness (justification). In Christ we are consecrated and set free (see 1 Cor. 1:24-30). The church's responsibility is to celebrate this Event of God, to be transformed by it, to proclaim it, to live in terms of it, and to invite all others to do likewise. For in the communication of this Event, the living God is disclosed again and again.

To receive this powerful communication is not to receive a piece of information about God, but to receive God.[4] Emil Brunner affirms: "In his Word, God does not deliver to me a course of lectures in dogmatic theology, he does not submit to me or interpret for me the content of a confession of faith, but he makes himself accessible to me. ... He does not communicate 'something' to me, but 'himself.' God is a person who himself speaks and discloses himself. ... An exchange takes place here which is wholly without analogy in the sphere of thinking. The sole analogy is in the encounter between human beings, the meeting of person with person."[5]

God is disclosed in the gospel as this gospel appears as indwelling Spirit in the life of the communicator, and as it is articulated in word and deed. Knowledge *about* God can be transmitted through books and tracts, but the personal knowledge *of* God is communicated through a vital, living testimony of self-revelation. Confrontation with God's self-disclosure in the gospel is what we mean by an encounter which demands response. Brunner called this "truth as encounter" and says, "In the Bible there encounters us now as formerly the truth of the God who came, is present, and will come to man. Faith is kindled, not by theology, but by the Word of God, by the history of the God who proclaims himself, and gives us a part with himself. ..."[6]

Martin Buber tells how he has often sat at his desk with books and papers before him, if not master, then at least manager in the realm of things; when all at once the telephone rings and a voice which he has never confused with any other voice says, "Martin, dinner is ready." In an instant the whole situation is transformed because a higher order of reality has cut across his existence. What is called for now is not so much reason as response to encounter.

So it is with Christian communication. It is more than a message; it is more than a system of intellectual thought; the Christian gospel is a message with a Messenger. Through the gospel, God is made accessible to us. Christian communication, therefore, evokes a discovery situation, a disclosure situation, a "John 3:19 situation," when the light of truth breaks through and people must choose between darkness and light. But what does it mean to say that the communication of God's Word leads to a disclosure situation of truth in Christ?

## THE CREATIVE WORD

God's Word is creative. "The Word is understood as creative power, like the Word of creation at the beginning. It effects what it says." [7] God's Word brings forth being out of nothing, thus transcending all analogies and all supposedly common things. Unlike the Greek understanding of *logos*, God's Word is not related to a being it discloses; rather it calls what is not into being (Rom. 4:17). "God speaks and it is done; God commands and it stands fast" (Psalm 33:9). God's Word creates light out of darkness and "Adam" from the dust of the soil; it establishes a nation in covenant and leads that nation into promise. It parents, prescribes, and founds. God's Word is Event that creates reality, action that obliges involvement, Person who cannot be ignored. Finally, God's Word is ultimately Jesus Christ, the unique and unavoidable saving Event in our history.

When this Word of God—the gospel—is faithfully communicated, it carries with it a creative power all its own. Paul said, "I am not ashamed of the gospel: *it* is the power of God for salvation to everyone who has faith." (Rom. 1:16). The power is in the gospel and not in the gospel communicator. "The Word of God is hence not verified against anything else, either the external events of history or the inner experiences of men; it verifies itself, enforces its own claims, illuminates through its own being." [8] It is the good news content of Christian proclamation that has the power to elicit response. The Word of God has its own way of addressing the human soul. It is not necessary to attempt to put power into it. "The Word moves of its own accord, and all the Christian communicator has to do is assist that movement and try to put no obstacles in its path. The Word comes forth to take people to itself." Bonhoeffer continues: "When this Word comes, the Holy Spirit comes showing to Christians individually and corporately, the gifts of the incarnate Christ. . . . He produces faith in his hearers, that they may discern in the preaching the entry of Jesus Christ." [9]

Let us now look at this communication of the living God. In the previous chapter we observed that the living God is one who speaks, who creates, who is interested in and committed to creation, who takes initiative and acts on behalf of creation. Thus, Christianity puts great emphasis upon God's involvement in history. In Leviticus we read where God says to the people, "I will make my dwelling with you" (Lev. 26:11). The psalmist picked this up when he said, "God is our refuge and strength, a very present help in time of trouble" (Psalm 46). The prophets reiterated the same message when they spoke of God's steadfast love and presence with Israel. Ezekiel has God saying, "My dwelling place will be with them; and I will be their God and they will be my people" (Ezek. 37:27). It is the intent of God to be present with creation.

But the Old Testament message of God's redeeming action did not break fully upon the world. Clearly, for the eternal Word of God to become more understandable to people, God had to share to the full in the space-time world of human existence, within the finite conditions of created life.[10] So, God took drastic measures and wrapped up the Word in a Person and "The Word became flesh and dwelt among us." And "we called him Emmanuel, meaning, God with us" (John 1:14; Matt. 1:23). Paul used the word *kenosis* (emptying) in Philippians 2:7 to speak of this communicative action of God in Christ: Christ, who was in the form of God, "emptied himself." He became the fully human embodiment of God's gracious purpose to save us. According to this passage, the result of the emptying was that Christ became like us in our human situation. Incarnation means that God approaches us in our own frame of reference.

The incarnation with its account of the birth of Jesus to a simple people, in a humble, lonely place of ordinary human circumstances, is a paradigm of God's method of communication: not through a magic emergence of a full-grown hero god straight from the head of Zeus (as Athena was said to have been born), nor through spectacular pomp and circumstance, but in a tiny babe in whom the "hopes and fears of all the years are met." The baby's name is Jesus, which again underscores the point that incarnation is basic to God's saving action. Jesus, which is the Greek form of "Joshua," means "Yahweh will save." But the name also marks Jesus' coming as an infant, placing him historically and geographically. As Paul wrote to the Galatians, he was not only born of woman but he was "born under the law" (Gal. 4:4). He dwelt among us in humility and servitude. He spoke profound truth in a simple fashion. He knew family life; worked with his hands; associated with the sick, the disenfranchised, the ostracized, the powerless as well as the rich and the powerful, the profane as well as the devout.

Jesus' own being was formed in such a way that his message and his relationships were the vehicle of divine self-communication. He "embodied" the intention of God, both in his person and in his proclamation of the kingdom. During his lifetime, his followers grasped only fragments of his decisive role in the reconciliation of humankind, but with his death, resurrection, and appearances, his ministry and interpretation of the kingdom were seen as vindicated by God. His life and ministry were thrown into a new light. He was not just a messenger; he was the Message itself (2 Cor. 5:16-21).[11] Because of the resurrection, the Jesus who preached has become the Jesus who *is* preached; he who brought the message has become the content of the message. Jesus Christ in terms of his life, death, and resurrection has become the sum and substance of the message of the kingdom of God and the key to the meaning of history. "There is hence no fundamental difference between the proclamation of Jesus and the proclamation of the Church. Through His history itself, Jesus' gospel about the Kingdom of God became the Church's gospel about Jesus, the Christ of God." [12]

Now the gospel is the good news of God's breakthrough to humanity. His truth, love, and righteousness have come into life and are made available for redemption and reconciliation. This makes clear that the gospel is more than a verbal communication, more than a set of theological affirmations or ethical rules. The gospel includes the method by which God communicates and is made known. God does not speak one way and act another. Words and deeds are one. Message and method, content and relationship are linked in the gospel. Therefore, we cannot share Word without sharing world. Communication and communion are inseparably tied in Christian communication.

This inherent balance in authentic Christian communication ought to help us to shy away from forms of communication based upon inflexible slogans and gimmicks, and it ought to constrain us to involve ourselves sensitively in the real dilemmas of real people. How else can we follow the one who takes "upon himself the form of a servant and dwells among us"? (Phil. 2). The one called "Emmanuel" certainly didn't bombard people with slogans, tracts, and high-powered media campaigns. He walked the roads with people. Without relationship our words and slogans are little more than chatter. Without relationship the Christian communicator becomes a peddler of words.

But, on the other hand, this inherent balance in authentic Christian communication will not allow us to play down communication by words. Words are indispensable. Word, language, and speech are a substantial part of proclaiming the revelation of God to humanity. "And God *said* . . .," introduces the events of creation. The prophets *spoke* in the name of God. Jesus not only came as the Word made flesh, but he spoke his message to the people. He "came preaching the kingdom of God." After Jesus' death and resurrection the disciples "came preaching" the good news. The church has always depended upon the spoken word.

## THE GOSPEL STORY

Since the gospel is the good news of God's breakthrough to humanity, it is necessary to turn to a consideration of how that gospel took shape. Two thousand years ago, a small band of people went out into the streets of the cities and towns of the Greco-Roman world to tell an amazing story. They called this story "gospel," the good news of salvation. They were on fire with the message of this story and they proclaimed it fearlessly. This story had to do with something new that God had done, something which changed everything, something which turned the world upside-down. Today, in the last decades of the twentieth century, Christians continue to sing, "We've a Story to Tell to the Nations." What is that story and how did it take shape?

Rushing into a quick and easy answer to this question would be a mistake, for there is a bewildering variety of attempts to formulate both the content and the contours of the Christian story. Biblical scholars and church historians are constantly reminding us of the diversity of formulations in the Bible and in Christian tradition. One gets the impression of a multiplicity of stories rather than a single story. Moreover, the heavy emphasis upon historical relativity (that is, what we believe is always shaped by historical-cultural contexts and heredity) makes our efforts to get to the heart of the story seem suspect if not illegitimate. On the one hand, part of this is due to the fact that the presentations of the gospel in the New Testament itself are culturally conditioned. The report of God's self-revelation in scriptures was given in terms of the writer's own culture. On the other hand, part of this can be seen in the fact that the biblical writers not only made use of the historical and cultural materials available to them, but they also wrote from varying theological perspectives. In addition, our own history, theology, and culture will influence our interpretation. None of us approaches the scriptures out of a cultural or theological vacuum. We cannot jump out of our own skin. We come to the scriptures from our own particular ethnic, sexual, geographic, theological, and socioeconomic perspectives.

I shall attempt to honor this view of the Christian story

without allowing it to muzzle the storyteller or displace the basic content of the message. First, I shall do this by filing a disclaimer: this attempt to get at the basic content of the story lays no claim to a "God's eye point of view." Like all statements of faith, it is a translation-interpretation. I simply mean to say that there are no moments in which the "pure" story is told. As the story is appropriated, articulated, and passed on, it is already caught up in reflection and brought into relation to one's own concepts and self-understanding, to the questions and crises of one's own existential situation, to the situation of the hearers and much else besides. Therefore, when a person tells the story there is a sense in which it is always presented in interpreted form. "Any version of Christianity produced anywhere at any time will bear marks of one-sidedness or myopia not only because of imperfect exegesis and theologizing but also for reasons of cultural limitations. A culture operates as both binoculars and blinkers, helping you to see some things and keeping you from seeing others." [13]

But, second, I do not believe the basic Christian story gets shipwrecked just because it is expressed in terms of one's own stream of history, nor do I believe that the heart of that message is in any sense a slave to cultural pluralism. The basic point and unity of the story remains behind the diversity in theological and cultural perspective. I agree with Gabriel Fackre: "There is an out-thereness of biblical truth which is to be seen, whatever the angle of vision [perspective], and however our view of it is affected by the glasses we are wearing. There is an object with which our subjectivity deals. There is a Story which our translation seeks to communicate. There is a hard-core of affirmation at the center of our perceptions and interpretations." [14] If this were not the case, then we would have to choose between the various theologies offered in the scripture, and this would further bifurcate the Body of Christ. We should then be disciples of John, Paul, or Matthew, but not biblical Christians. We should then ascribe to our particular version of the gospel a finality and universality which would not only do an injustice to the biblical record but would ultimately impair the spread of the gospel and the growth of the church.

The heart of the Christian story is set within the broader context of a living tradition which recounts the history of God's dealings with the human family. In other words, though the Christian story centers upon the Event of Jesus Christ, it is clear that God's action in Christ does not stand alone. It cannot be properly understood without constant reference to the whole story of God's activity, past, present, and future. For the Christian, the Event of God in Jesus Christ is the focusing center from which we view the deeper meaning of the whole story of God's dealings with the human family. This suggests what can be called a reciprocal influence in interpretation: The complete story is necessary in order to interpret the central chapter, and the central chapter is necessary in interpreting the whole story. In other words, while the divine activity is not confined to God's revelation in Christ, the wider range of God's activity is defined by the Christ-Event. Here, let us review some of the wider traditions in which the story of Christ is the central chapter.

The Christian story is a story about God's vision of *shalom*. The Hebrew word *shalom* attempts to embody the biblical vision of God's central, full, and ultimate intention for all creation. "In the beginning" God had a vision of a world of peace, justice, freedom, wholeness, and well being. The unfolding of salvation history traces God's struggle to establish this reconciling peace *(shalom)*, freedom, and wholeness with humanity, among humankind, within persons and between human beings and nature. It is out of this vision that God created. All existence came into being through the instrumentality of the Divine Word, "Let there be. . . ." Therefore, there was an integrity to God's creation, for God intended that all created things should remain in harmonious relation to each other and to their Creator.

Persons were created in God's image and were intended to be the historic actors who live in and for the Creator's vision of *shalom*. That is, being in God's image, human beings were created to be in relation to God and to one another and not in isolation. Reflecting the relational nature of God, humans were created as relational beings. To be human, therefore, is to be in relation. "Male and female, sister and brother, self and neighbor,

are the human polarities that in relation define our humanity." [15]
In creation God allowed that humans should have the freedom to
say yes or no to the divine vision. And here the plot thickens! We
prove to be far more interested in our own visions than in God's.
Therefore, we abuse our freedom, set ourselves against God and
one another, create systems that benefit only the most privileged
among us, and, contrary to the God-given structure of life,
namely, its relational character, we allow our selfish actions to
take control and we become estranged from nature, ourselves, each
other, and God. Therefore, the divine image given in creation
becomes distorted and defaced and our lives are given over to
contradictions of the very structure of existence. God's dream and
intention of *shalom* meets its deepest resistance in the human
being.

Hearing the story of what happened in the creation and fall
connects so forcefully with the realities of our present existence.
Is it not true that what was said to have been an event then is also
an account of what takes place right now? Adam's (meaning
humankind's) saga is ours! Humanity falls, but what does the fall
mean? "The fall of humanity means that *sin* is our response to the
invitation from God. Sin is the code word in the Christian Story
for the turning inward of the self, and, thus, the turning away
from God, neighbor, and nature. It is the use of our freedom to
serve ourselves rather than the employment of that freedom in
the service of God and in the Divine purpose. Sin is an 'ego trip'
inward rather than a pilgrimage outward and ahead toward the
horizon of Shalom (Rom. 8:7)." [16]

But God's love goes on reaching and seeking. God calls a people
into being, a people to witness to the divine vision. God called
Abraham to go out into a new land to establish a new people who
would express the Creator's purpose. Isaac, Jacob, and Joseph,
descendants of Abraham, were called to express God's divine intention. After Joseph's death, there came to power those who "did
not know Joseph," and the people of Israel were enslaved in
Egypt. Then God called Moses to liberate the people from oppression and develop them into a new covenant people for a new land.
The covenant call to be God's people was not a call to special

rights but to special responsibility. The people of God were responsible to be a "light to the nations" (Isa. 49:6). They were to witness before the nations to the God of *shalom*.

In the history of the covenanted people, God continued to seek to share the divine vision. Persons such as Deborah, Amos, and Isaiah were called to keep God's will and mercy before the people and their leaders. Israel was to be a representative people, a people where the Lord's reign was to be seen from the far ends of the earth. As a covenant people they were challenged to live a distinctively different life than the other nations of the world. Therefore, the law, expressing the ethical content of the covenant, was given. But, again, God's action and vision were thwarted, for the people turned to disobedience and idolatry. God continued to raise up prophets to keep alive a faithful remnant who would not lose sight of their Creator's vision. But the people "stoned the messengers and the prophets" (Luke 13:14). Still God did not give up. God would not be finished with history and history's people until justice and righteousness "roll down like waters" and God's vision is complete (Amos 5:24).

The depth of human sin, however, "required a correspondingly deep plunge into a resisting world issuing in the suffering Love at the center of human history, Jesus Christ." [17] So, God acts again, entering our human condition, becoming incarnate in Jesus of Nazareth. As Fackre puts it, "*Shalom* is born at Bethlehem, lives in Galilee. In Him hope happens. He is our liberator, our peace, the light of the world." [18] Through Jesus the good news of the kingdom is announced. Through Jesus God lives our life, takes our flesh, and puts himself into our hands. But, in our sin and rebellion, we nail the ultimate expression of God's love to a rugged cross. However, in the act of dying upon the cross Jesus manifests the awesome love of God delivering us from bondage to the principalities and powers. In the resurrection God proves that it is love and not any worldly power or force that makes the world go round. God proves that it is love that is the first principle of the universe.

Just as the good news of God's deliverance was found in the call of Abraham, the Exodus, the creation of Israel, in the divine mercy that would not leave Israel alone but kept turning disaster into discipline, so that good news of God's deliverance reached its consummation in the dawn of the new age in Jesus of Nazareth and his victory of life over death, love over hate, reconciliation over alienation. Gabriel Fackre gives us the following summary of the work of Jesus Christ in the salvation of the world:

What did Christ do? He brought us at-one-ment, liberation from sin, evil and death, and reconciliation with God, neighbor and nature. How?

He saw and shared the vision of God. He was the Prophet who perceived and pointed to the horizon light of God's *Shalom*. A Prophet, but more than a prophet, for the Light that shown toward him also shown *in* him. The Vision became flesh and manifested itself in deeds of liberation and reconciliation.

He was a Seer, but also a Sufferer, a Priest as well as a Prophet. He suffered for the vision of God, exposing the hate of the world as it sought to extinguish the Light of God, and so, too, he suffered the sight of the eclipse of the sun of *Shalom*, obedience unto death. And he was the embodied vision of God that suffered that death, and in that suffering took into the Divine life our punishment, releasing the mercy that covers our sin.

He was the Seer and Sufferer, but also the Liberator and Lord. The sword of the cross pierced the armor of the powers and principalities. The risen Christ is the Conqueror who opens the future and assures the coming of the Kingdom. No more do we fear the thrones and authorities that rattle their swords in this world, for they have met their match, and we are empowered to resist them in the liberation and reconciliation struggles of our time, even as we meet the last enemy, death, in hope. "Thanks be to God who has given us the victory through our Lord Jesus Christ!" [19]

The message of the kingdom, on the lips of Jesus, was the good news that God's sovereign reign or rule was beginning. In the latter teachings of the Old Testament "kingdom" came to refer to a definite state of time when all things would be subjected to God. In the advent and ministry of Jesus Christ this decisive reign of God has its dawning. A new age dawns and the urgency of entering the new age pulsates in the message of Jesus: "The time is fulfilled and the Kingdom of God is at hand" (Mark 1:15). Jesus' invitation is to enter God's kingdom, with the consequence that a radical new relationship with God is established. To enter the kingdom of God requires that we repent of our citizenship in the old age and turn around toward the new. While the consummation of the new age is to come, the power of the new age is already operative in the ministry of Jesus. The blind see, the deaf hear, the lame walk, and the poor receive the gospel.

Thus, Jesus' invitation to the kingdom is an invitation to a new life characterized by repentance, faith, and loving obedience. Those who enter the kingdom are those who have turned from the old world of bondage to principalities and powers and have placed their trust in God. As members of God's kingdom they are to live for God and for other people. In keeping with the ethical content of repentance in the Old Testament, Jesus summarized the law and the prophets by demanding unqualified love for God and for the neighbor (Matt. 22:37-40). Therefore, throughout the New Testament the ethical norm is to love others in the same manner in which God has unconditionally, indiscriminantly loved the human race.[20]

## THE NEW ISRAEL

In the birth, life, crucifixion, and resurrection of Jesus of Nazareth, God acts in suffering love, inviting all of creation to accept the blessings and responsibilities of the kingdom of God. Some hear the call and are changed from God's enemies into friends and are given the task of sharing God's truth with the world. Thus, God calls into being a new people, a new community responsible to live with their Creator and with one another in a fellowship of covenant love and loyalty. This community of faith becomes the New Israel. It is a new messianic community in which Jew and Gentile are together as fellow citizens, branches of one olive tree and brothers and sisters in one family. The Spirit of the risen Christ indwells them and they find themselves participating in a new creation, a new order of redeemed relationships set in the midst of the old order of broken relationships.

Through the gift of the Holy Spirit at Pentecost (Acts 2), this community is empowered to witness to God's saving activity. Therefore, at Pentecost a missionary community is born; the Holy Spirit empowers this community with the gifts necessary to participate in God's mission in the world. This new messianic community begins to spread the Christian story throughout the world. They live and move in the conviction that the risen Christ is available to everyone and at every geographical point, as a matter of fact, knocking at every human door (Rev. 3:20). Being filled with the Holy Spirit they go forth to spread the gospel.

Here is the first gospel sermon, preached by Peter: "This zeal and enthusiasm which you see," to paraphrase his words, "has come because the promises made to the Old Testament prophets are being fullfilled. God has sent his Spirit upon us, so that we may preach the mighty working by which he has redeemed the world. You know of Jesus of Nazareth, whom your rulers crucified. That same Jesus, who was sent forth from God and approved among you by the signs which he performed, has now by God's mighty act been raised from the dead. Because he is risen, he has shed forth the Holy Spirit; and in the power of the Spirit, we are sent out to call people to repentance and to acceptance of Jesus as Lord of all and redeemer of the world" (Acts 2). On another occasion (Acts 5:30-32), Peter declared, "The God of our fathers raised up Jesus, whom you had done to death by hanging him on a gibbet. He it is whom God has exalted with his own right hand as leader and Savior, to grant Israel repentance and forgiveness of sins. And we are witnesses to all of this" (NEB).

Again, Peter says of Jesus that God anointed him "with the Holy Spirit and with power. He went about doing good and healing all who were oppressed by the devil, for God was with him. And we can bear witness to all that he did in the Jewish countryside and in Jerusalem. He was put to death by hanging on a gibbet; but God raised him to life on the third day, and allowed him to appear, . . . and he commanded us to proclaim him to the people, and affirm that he is the one who has been designated by God as the judge of the living and the dead. It is to him that all the prophets testify, declaring that everyone who trusts in him receives forgiveness of sins through his name" (Acts 10:38-43).

## THE HEART OF THE MATTER

This, then, represents the heart or core of the earliest preaching of the good news. It was not so much information about God's nature as proclamation of God's action. It was the affirmation that God had done something new and wonderful: God had acted in and through Jesus of Nazareth, so that whoever believes in him receives remission of sins. Therefore, life receives a new meaning, people are empowered from on high, a new creation is established by God's deed. This was the gospel: the good news that in Jesus God had visited and redeemed people.

For these early Christians the gospel was not a little bit of everything. It was not a general lesson in morals and good conduct. For them, the gospel was very specific "good news." Now the shape of the gospel varied somewhat in terms of particular backgrounds and particular contexts, and there was rich diversity of theological formulation in early New Testament preaching. However, despite diversity, there was a basic apostolic content to the witness. It ran something like this: The new age has dawned; God has acted directly in the life and the death and resurrection of Jesus Christ. All this is the fulfillment of prophecy, and the very conception of prophecy implies a vision and plan that are being steadily worked out in the world. This Jesus who lived and died in the world will come again. Meanwhile, the company of those who believe in him is marked off as the New Israel of God, uniquely God's people by the gift of the Holy Spirit. In the name of Christ forgiveness and new life are offered to people. Therefore, all are called to turn and trust the living God revealed in the gospel.

The letters of Paul are certainly based on this theme, although the apostle approaches and states the theme in many different ways. The first four books of the New Testament are called Gospels, because they tell this story of good news. Mark, for example, informs us that he tells the story of Jesus' early ministry as the beginning of the gospel of Jesus Christ, the Son of God. John writes his Gospel in order that people might believe that Jesus is the Christ, the Son of God; and that believing they might have life through his name.

This basic apostolic witness is foundational to any understanding of Christian conversion. Allowing room for contextualizations, the church must proclaim: (1) God has acted in Jesus Christ to reinstitute fellowship with himself. (2) The rule of sin is destroyed at its roots. (3) People must turn from every destructive way and toward God. (4) As the sign of this new age, people will receive the Holy Spirit, God for us today and our guarantee of the total fulfillment of all God's promises. The thrust of this message is reconciliation to God, the point of the whole drama of salvation both for individuals and for all creation. The call is to leave behind the kingdom of sin, of corruption, and evil, for the rule of God, for life, righteousness, and justice. This New Testament message, therefore, is a call to relationship necessitating a radical dissatisfaction with our present life, a radical transformation given by God, yet requiring our response. This call to believe, repent, and receive, is also a call to a new way of existence; it is a call to discipleship.

Wherever the "heart" of the gospel of Christ is fervently proclaimed and lived, the conditions are ripe for Christian conversion to happen. Paul says that "Faith is awakened by the message, and the message that awakens it comes through the Word of Christ" (Rom. 10:17). This is another way of saying that that which triggers turning and trusting is the message; the discovery of the good news that the life, death, and resurrection of Christ heralds the demise of the powers of darkness; the discovery that in Christ God has come to the people; in Christ a new age has dawned; the powers of evil, sin, and death have met their master; in Christ a new heaven has begun its descent to a new earth; the kingdoms of this world have met a superior kingdom; in Christ we know by anticipation the end *(telos)* of history. Not that we have reached the end of history or the end of conflict, but that we know what the end is and the certainty of its triumphant issue.

Thus, these historic acts of God provide a new perspective for the eyes of faith, a new ground of certainty, a new view of God's purposes, and a new sense of God's power. In the life, death, and resurrection of Jesus Christ and in the empowering which began at Pentecost, God has spoken uniquely. As a result, two factors are made accessible: adequate knowledge of God's purpose and adequate power to respond. These are accessible not because people have become righteous through their own power, but because God has initiated a new movement of saving activity in Jesus Christ.

The essence of evangelizing lies in the faithful presentation of this gospel by word and deed. The noun form of "gospel" is *euangelion*. This word is also the root of our term *evangelizing*. It is impossible to talk about the gospel without talking about evangelizing, and, likewise, it is impossible to talk about evangelizing without the gospel. If it is the spread of the gospel which constitutes evangelizing, then the gospel is utterly normative, and there is no Christian conversion without it. Barth did not overstate the case when he said, "It is unequivocally and exclusively by the Gospel, the revealed grace of God, that conversion is effectively commanded as a radical termination and a radical recommencement." [21] This is why the apostle Paul insists that the gospel is "the power of God for salvation . . . for in it the righteousness of God is revealed" (Rom. 1:16-17). Notice that he does not say that the gospel is *about* God's power, but it *is* God's power.

Leander Keck gives a revealing exegesis of this Pauline passage. He reminds us that the gospel was the power of God not because it was a piece of revealed theology. Paul was not a Gnostic. The gospel is neither about God's power nor is it God's power in the sense of information with saving power. It is God's power because of what happens in connection with it. The righteousness of God is revealed in it (Rom. 1:16-17). Notice that Paul does not say that God's righteousness was once revealed, and that the gospel is a news item about it. If Paul had written that, he would have implied that the revelation of God's righteousness is a past event, and that the gospel is a report about what happened once upon a time, somewhere else. Paul surely does not doubt the importance of what happened in the Event of Jesus in the past. But what he insists on is that this revelatory Event keeps on revealing. The revelation keeps on occurring from faith to faith. This means that wherever the gospel is preached and believed something happens which is more than just a split off the original revelation.

What Paul is driving at is that the gospel is not just a report of a revelation which had occurred in Jesus Christ, but that where the gospel is preached and lived, there, too, revelation occurs. Thus, when Paul says, "The righteousness of God is revealed," he means that it was revealed in the Event of Jesus Christ and now stands revealed for all who believe. Believers know that it was revealed once because it continues to be revealed in them and for them. This helps us see that what happens in the proclamation of the gospel is a revelation which participates in the original revelation. Therefore, the decisive revelation in Jesus Christ is not far away, long ago—but right now!

This is true because God raised Jesus from the dead, and the resurrection is more than a mere miracle, a stupendous event which happened in the past. To the contrary, the resurrection is an eschatological event, a sign of the new age, the clue that another reality is breaking in. Jesus Christ *is* alive! Whoever believes *that* must confess Jesus as Lord, as the hallmark of ultimate reality and the one to whom we are ultimately accountable.

Were it not for the resurrection, we would have no choice but to preach Jesus as example, law, or obligation. But, there is no good news in that! The demand to be like Jesus or to do what he says is only the intensification of the law. Where people cease to believe the resurrection or else treat it as a miracle of the past, they also tend to preach Jesus within the context of works righteousness. Therefore, instead of being a gift of God's wondrous love, Jesus becomes another Moses who makes impossible demands on top of the ones we already have. Such a message cannot reveal the righteousness of God which was disclosed in Christ. For the righteousness of God disclosed in Christ features a God who acts on behalf of persons who fail to measure up to the law. The distinction of the gospel is that it offers salvation precisely to those who fail to measure up to the standards of the law.

But the resurrection made Jesus Christ as alive as God and as directly accessible as God. Therefore, wherever the message of the gospel is proclaimed, the living Lord makes happen again what happened originally. Now we can understand how Paul can say that the gospel is not simply a piece of information about the past, nor is it simply a piece of doctrine about God's power. It is rather the means, the instrument, by which God's power is revealed for those who believe.

To summarize: The gospel is not a report about God's power but an event in which God's power becomes operative when it is believed. This is because in the preaching and believing of the gospel, God's righteousness is not God's fairness by which God gives everyone what is deserved, but God's act of setting things right precisely where no one deserves it. For in the gospel a revelation of God's true character happens, a character set forth in the event called Jesus Christ.[22]

It is the widespread loss of confidence in the truth, power, and relevance of the gospel of Jesus Christ which impedes the growth of the contemporary church. For not only is the gospel of the kingdom the saving power of God, it is also that which energizes the church with expectancy and hope. Without the message of the gospel of the kingdom, life cannot be lived in joy, expectancy, and hope. And without the note of joy, expectancy, and hope, the church gives an uncertain sound and her members do not gird themselves for service in the world. They grow weary in well doing. They suffer "compassion fatigue." One of the most incessant tasks of our day is to kindle the true hope of the gospel of the kingdom, for lack of which people pursue the will-of-the-wisps of secular illusion, whose fruit is ashes and whose end is despair.

The church lives only as it communicates the gospel. As Jürgen Moltmann reminds us, "The Christian Church grew out of the apostolic proclamation of the Gospel and is alive in the act of proclamation. . . ." [23] This means that it is possible for the church to cease to be a church, to lose the gospel, to cool off by loss of the Spirit's presence, and to become secularized to the point of being nothing more than an imitation of the world. The Christian faith has a particular content. It makes a particular claim to truth, and that is that the all-fulfilling future of humankind and the world's salvation has already arrived in its initial phase in Jesus, the Jew from Nazareth. Any church that ceases to affirm this Event and to live out its meaning has ceased to be a Christian community.

Moreover, I repeat, there can be no Christian conversion without the gospel. Christian conversion doesn't happen by simply talking about it, though we do need to articulate our thoughts and share ideas with regard to conversion. It doesn't happen by analyzing it, though it is important to understand the biblical, theological, psychological, and ethical dimension of conversion.[24] Christian conversion doesn't happen by doing word studies, though we need to be clear about the language of our faith and need to be alert to new idioms that communicate Christian truth. Christian conversion happens when the gospel is communicated and when there is response to it. It is only the person who trusts God as the gospel presents God who experiences Christian conversion.

We have seen how the living God initiates conversion and makes it possible, but now it is necessary to turn to a consideration of the nature of the human being and the human response. For the music of Christian conversion comes from a string drawn taut between two points: divine initiative and human response (Phil. 3:12).

## QUESTIONS FOR THOUGHT AND DISCUSSION

1. A recurring theme in this chapter is that God does not communicate divine information to us; God communicates God! Can you give an example from your own life of the personal self-revelation of God?

2. On page 69 the author quotes Gabriel Fackre's answer to the question, "What did Christ do?" Can you personalize this? What does Christ do *for you*?

3. Reread the section on "The New Israel" with your own congregation in mind. How does your church compare with this New Testament picture of the church?

4. Based on this chapter, how would you express "the heart of the gospel" in one paragraph? One sentence? One word?

5. The author says, "There can be no Christian conversion without the gospel." How would you describe the function of the gospel as you've summarized it (4 above) in conversion?

# 6. Who Needs Conversion and Why?

As you have followed the outline of this book so far, perhaps you are asking, "Why wait until now to speak of the human predicament, of our human nature? Is the cure not worked out in relation to the disease? Why speak of the love of God and the good news of salvation before establishing an understanding of the human flaw which causes us to need both?"

All of us know that the question of salvation cannot be separated from the perception of the human dilemma, and that a superficial reading of the human sickness generally results in only symptomatic cures. However, I began with God's revelation because God is prior and the gospel is normative. This being the case, any real knowledge of ourselves both in terms of the seriousness of our sin and the possibility of salvation are, alike, the results of God's initiative, God's revelation.

It is God who reveals to us who we really are and what we really need. In an encounter with God it is human beings who are known, and who know themselves as objects of God's knowledge. The important thing here is not so much what we can know or intuit by our own powers, but the fact that God takes the initiative in approaching and knowing us. Fortunately, God does not wait for us to come to an understanding of ourselves through technical research and then come for help.

Through the gospel God reveals to us the kind of people we are, the kind of world we live in, and the kind of world that lives in us. Through the mighty action of God the world and the human condition are unmasked and seen for what they are. Only by way of God's revelation can we know that we are sinners, rebels against

God's love and God's vision of *shalom*. We could never have known this had it not been for God's action in the history of Israel, and especially, in Jesus' death on the cross. Whatever else the cross teaches, it certainly makes transparent the fact that our sin is so deep that we cannot stand to have God too close. The cross is evidence of our radical and total estrangement from God. If the cross is taken seriously, it is no longer possible to think unrealistically about human potential or to expect salvation to come from our own powers and abilities.

The fact that we know something of sin and its impact is evidence that we have had some kind of encounter with God and have been given a criterion for evaluating the human condition. In other words, for the Christian, knowledge of the human condition is "faith knowledge." From this unique knowledge we learn that sin goes far deeper and is more comprehensive than what we can dig up out of our own lives through self-analysis. In self-analysis we tend to compare ourselves with ourselves, our performance with our conscience, our conduct with our ideal of what we would like to be. This can, and often does, lead to a confirmation of ourselves in the light of ourselves; and this is a form of absolutizing the self! But the gospel does more than confirm; it calls us into question. It does more than express us; it exposes us in the light of God's holiness and love.

The scriptures contain countless illustrations of how an encounter with God heightens the awareness of sin. Persons who have caught a glimpse of God's glory have also gotten an overwhelming consciousness of their own sin. When God appeared to Moses, Moses "hid his face for he was afraid to look at God" (Ex. 3:1-6). When God spoke to Job out of the whirlwind, Job responded by saying, "I had heard of thee by the hearing of the ear, but now my eyes see thee; therefore I despise myself and repent in dust and ashes" (Job 42:5-6, RSV). When Isaiah encountered God in the temple he cried out, "Woe is me! I am lost; for I am a man of unclean lips, and dwell among a people of unclean lips" (Isa. 6:1-5). When Ezekiel received his unusual vision and felt that he recognized in the one on the throne the appearance of the likeness of the glory of the Lord he said, "When I saw it, I fell upon my face" (Ezek. 1:26-28, RSV).

When Saul of Tarsus confronted the risen Christ on the Damascus road he was struck to the ground and blinded (Acts 9:1-9). When John on the Island of Patmos confronted a vision of the risen and glorified Christ he said, "When I saw him, I fell at his feet as though dead" (Rev. 1:9-17). A vision of our own predicament follows any encounter with the living God. God reveals to us the sinfulness of sin. Had it not been for divine initiative David would have remained in his sin, for it is sin which is the source of blindness. However, through the prophet Nathan, God enabled David to see the exceeding sinfulness of his life (2 Sam. 12).

Karl Barth goes so far as to insist that people come to know their sin exclusively through confrontation with Christ. In the light of Christ's humiliation our existence is revealed in its pride. In the light of Christ's exultation, our condition is seen in terms of its sloth. In the light of Christ's disclosure of truth, our existence is seen in terms of its untruthfulness. For Barth, sin is in its unity and totality always and simultaneously pride, sloth, and lying, which are always and simultaneously opposed to the self-humiliation of God, to the glorification of Christ, and to the witness of the God-man. In this way sin always and simultaneously manifests unbelief and disobedience. Barth's observations concerning sin as pride are especially telling: Jesus Christ the Son of God becomes man; but the person of pride wants to be like God. Jesus Christ the Lord becomes servant; but we proud servants want to be lord. Jesus Christ the judge allows himself to be judged; but we want to be the judge ourselves. Jesus Christ helped us by becoming helpless on the cross and in the tomb; but we want to help ourselves.[1] Thus we come to know our true selves in confrontation with this Christ.

To insist that knowledge of our identity as sinners is "faith knowledge" is not to insinuate that other knowledge in the world is worthless. Obviously, other avenues to a genuine and deep awareness of ourselves can be found outside the Christian encounter with God. I am not saying that the knowledge that comes of God in Christ is exclusive; rather, it is normative. Therefore, knowledge of the human situation that comes through psychology and other technical fields can be affirmed, deepened, and clarified by the Christian knowledge of sin. To say that the gospel is normative is to affirm that the truth about human nature is revealed only if we look at it through the lens of the gospel, and what the gospel reveals is not simply identical with what social science or social criticism reveals, though there may be considerable overlap. But one simply cannot begin with social criticism or psychological interpretation and then declare, "This is what the gospel says." Because, what the gospel reveals is a faith perception. It is not the result of self-analysis or poll-taking.

Therefore, the Christian simply cannot accept at face value the world's own self-understanding. To do so would result in taking the world's self-diagnosis and declaring that what the world is looking for is what the gospel offers. In resistance to this shallow notion, Thomas Merton says:

Adaptation to society at best helps a man "to live with his illness rather than cure it," particularly if the general atmosphere of the society is unhealthy because of its over-emphasis on cerebral, competitive, acquisitive forms of ego affirmation. Such an atmosphere may favor an apparently very active and productive mode of life but in reality it stifles true growth, leaves people lost, alienated, frustrated and bored without any way of knowing what is wrong with them. In fact, in many cases, psychoanalysis has become a technique for making people conform to a society that prevents them from growing and developing as they should.[2]

According to the gospel, the world knows what it wants, but it does not know what it needs. To offer the gospel as an answer to what the world wants is to pander to selfishness and avarice. The world simply does not understand itself rightly nor does it know what it is looking for. It is this capacity of the gospel to reveal ourselves to ourselves that must be recovered. As Helmut Thielicke has said, "Identity is riveted to God's Word."[3]

What the gospel reveals about our nature as sinners is uncommonly hard and radical. It would be beyond endurance were it not for our faith that the God who comes to us does so lovingly, forgivingly, and renewingly. God sees through us and yet God loves us. It is in the light of God's grace that we are told the truth about ourselves. Standing in the light of God's grace, manifested in Christ, we can bear to look into the dark corners of our lives, and we discover that the gospel not only discloses the self; it transforms the self. But, conversely, this message of forgiveness and renewal cannot be understood if we are unwilling to accept how radically we need forgiveness and renewal. In summary, knowledge of the human situation apart from the gospel is impotent. But the gospel apart from an understanding of its correlation to the human predicament is meaningless. What does the gospel tell us about the human situation?

## A SERIOUS PREDICAMENT

Our family has a camera that must be focused before each picture is taken. There is nothing automatic about it! It takes beautiful colored slides when focused properly, but the pictures are always blurred when taken out of focus. According to the Christian gospel, our lives are fundamentally out of focus. Moreover, we are utterly helpless to "focus" our lives properly. If correct focus is to come, it must come from a power beyond us.

To put it in more traditional language, sin has affected us at the very core of our existence. Therefore, we cannot make things right by merely readjusting, controlling, or reorganizing our own lives. Actually, this is part of the root problem. Instead of accepting God's power to focus our lives properly, we try to play God. We make self the center of our life. We overestimate our selves and our powers. We think we can manage our lives by rearranging some of the outward circumstances that affect us. But this only treats the symptoms and leaves the disease untouched. For it is at our very center that we must be "focused," that is, brought in line with God's purpose for our lives.[4]

How did the human family become so out of focus? As already stated, the human being was created as a "risky" being. A creature with a relational-personal nature and grounded in love must be given the possibility to refuse love or to bestow love, even to love the wrong things. The gospel teaches us that this possibility has become the "norm" for the human being, and this norm is so fatal that God's saving action in history is a continuous reaction to this abuse of freedom and a continuous struggle to conquer sin and carry forward God's purposes.

We were created with a need to find our focus—our very being—in the love of God. But we choose to find that focus elsewhere. In refusing God, an infinite number of other idolatrous possibilities open up. We can focus our existence on almost anything. However, all of these possibilities seem to swing between two poles. First, when we refuse to find our focus in God we may try to find it in the world. Paul spoke of this attempt to pull transcendence down into creation when he said, "They exchanged the glory of the immortal God for images resembling mortal man or birds or animals or reptiles" (Rom. 1:23 RSV). This is idolatry.

Second, when we refuse to find our focus in the living God we attempt to absolutize the self, to become an autonomous "I." Thus we proceed to insist that there is something within us—a divine spark or essence—something as divine as God is. This is the supreme illustration of our human arrogance, for it refuses to admit that we are "dust." This, likewise, is idolatry.

These two poles are helpful in our attempt to interpret the nature of sin. In the first instance we seek fulfillment in the world to which we give ourselves. In the second we become our own point of reference. At a glance we can see that these two poles are not extreme opposites but two sides of the same fundamental refusal to find our true focus in God. But the picture becomes even more complicated because, despite our sin, a kind of relationship to God continues to assert itself. We are apart from God and yet God's love will not let us go. Though estranged from God we continue to belong essentially to the One from whom we are estranged. As Augustine confessed, "Thou madest us for thyself, and our heart is restless, until it repose in Thee." [5] In estrangement the essential relationship to God doesn't disappear but becomes only an isolated element alongside other priorities, or else is sometimes used to achieve those priorities.[6]

This being "out of focus" is utterly serious and has life-or-death consequences. The gospel reveals sin in a radical way. We cling to our idols for the illusion of an acceptable self which those idols give, and we refuse to answer the calling of Christ or to discover the truth revealed in Christ. Having lost the central focus in life, we live our lives after the flesh, forever seeking outside stimulation. Being controlled by idols, we are not free to give of ourselves except where we hope to get. We are not free to value a thing or a person except where we hope for advantage to ourselves.

When people refuse to allow God to be the center of their lives, then selfishness with its isolation, emptiness, and loneliness, becomes their lot. They refuse God, and theirs becomes a life without high purpose, meaning, or hope. They let their lower self have its own way and eventually they discover that there is nothing left but death. There isn't any doubt but what "sin pays a wage, and the wage is death" (Rom. 6:23). George Buttrick speaks forceably about the serious nature of sin and our desperate need when he says, "We are constitutionally ignorant, indemically wicked, and irrevocably mortal. . . . We are ignorant, but we are aware of our ignorance, yet unable to lighten our darkness: We need a revelation. We are wicked, but know our wickedness, yet we cannot overcome it: We need a redemption. We are mortal and chained to mortality, though with a long enough chain to see it for what it is, yet we cannot break the chain: We need deliverance." [7]

This interpretation helps us understand that sin is more than transgression. It is bondage. It not only alienates us from God, it brings us into captivity. It is more than an unfortunate outward act or habit; it is a deep-seated inward condition. Martin Luther made this clear when he said, "Sin, in the Scripture, means not only the outward works of the body, but all the activities that move men to the outward works, namely, the inmost heart, with all its powers." [8] Sins of commission or omission (sloth) are but the visible manifestations of an inward or invisible condition.

Jesus' metaphors of the tree and its fruit are indicative of this. The kind of fruit a tree bears (olives or figs) and the condition of that fruit (whether good or bad) depend on the nature and health of the tree itself. Likewise, "A good man produces good from the store of good within himself; and an evil man from evil within produces evil. For the words that the mouth utters come from the overflow of the heart" (Luke 6:45). Again Jesus said, "For from inside, out of a man's heart, come evil thoughts, acts of fornication, of theft, murder, adultery, ruthless greed, and malice; fraud, indecency, envy, slander, arrogance, and folly; these evil things all come from inside, and they defile the man" (Mark 7:21-23). It is because of this inward condition that we are in bondage, and our bondage is not just a matter of certain acts or habits but the inward condition from which these spring. To quote Paul Tillich: "Sin is a universal fact before it becomes an individual act." [9]

John Wesley struggled with the question of sin as a deep-seated inward bondage. He had grown up with a religion of moral rectitude which had taught him that humans had the inward moral ability to refrain from sinning if they should choose to do so. Wesley did so choose and gave himself passionately to the goals of holy living. As a result of a number of events and influences throughout the year 1738, Wesley switched positions. He broke free from the religion of moral rectitude and embraced the gospel of justification by faith, which included a radically serious understanding of the universal human flaw—a flaw so serious that it is incurable by any human effort or merit. After 1738, Wesley held tenaciously to this Protestant diagnosis of the human predicament, original sin. Wesley understood original sin "as a malignant disease rather than the obliteration of the *imago Dei* in fallen human nature." [10] Therefore, he rejected the Lutheran and Calvinist doctrine of election in favor of his notion of prevenient grace—God's own continuous activity in calling sinners to repentance and new life and God's own power to cure the malignant disease that afflicts us. Wesley viewed sin "as a sickness that can be cured by the Great Physician." Though humans can do nothing to save themselves, this does not thwart the living God, "because it is God's purpose that the offer of grace shall be experienced as optional. The chief function of prevenient grace, therefore, is to stir the sinner to repentance." [11] The human responsibility is to accept God's three-fold prescription: (1) repentance, (2) renunciation of human merit, and (3) trust in God's unmerited grace.[12]

Given the serious nature of sin we need more than rules of conduct. A lecture on "Thou shalt nots" will not solve our problem. Anselm's comment is appropriate for those who assume that a person can be saved by laws, self-help efforts, or ethical virtues: "You have not yet considered the exceeding gravity of sin." [13] Because of the serious nature of sin, we need more than a system of generalized abstract propositions: we need a Saviour. An orphan boy doesn't need a book on motherhood. He doesn't need the latest insights in child psychology. He needs a mother! A woman trapped in her own private hell without knowing how to get out (and who of us hasn't been at one time or another) doesn't need a system of doctrinal propositions. This will not unlock the door. She needs a Saviour.[14] Only a Saviour can rescue us from such bondage. Only a Saviour can answer the deepest questions and needs of human existence.

Conversion, therefore, is a focal concern of the Christian faith because of the serious nature of our predicament. Only a radical reorientation (focusing) of life at its very center will suffice in the light of such great need. We must be changed within. If people are not "focused" correctly at the very center of their being, renewal of the world and renewal of personality are incomplete if not impossible.

## DIMENSIONS OF NEED

This need for "focusing," however, cannot be limited to the center of one's existence. The very nature of the gospel is such that it addresses itself to both individual and corporate sin, internal and external sin, and offers individual, corporate, internal, and external salvation. It is a total gospel which advocates total change (turning). Because sin has to do with the total of one's life, no piecemeal conversion will suffice. Life cannot be redeemed without, in some way, impacting everything that makes life what it is.

What good would it do to discover a new "focus" in terms of my inner life if that which makes me who and what I am remains unaffected? It would only succeed in calling me out of sinful social structures while leaving the structures themselves untouched. It would insinuate that our Lord is interested only in the individual sinner while ignoring the fallen orders of society. Since the structures of society are deeply infected with the sinful, selfish motives of people, my life cannot be brought into "focus" without challenging the evil structures which cramp and pervert my relationship to God, to people, to nature, and to my own self. Somehow, the question of human need must be put in such a way as to include all of these dimensions.

One characteristic of the Southern Appalachian region where I grew up is the constant encounter with religious road signs. Some signs read, "Prepare to meet thy God." Others: "Jesus is coming soon" (often chiseled in solid granite!). During a visit several summers ago I saw a sign that I had never seen. It read, "Christ is the answer." Immediately, I thought, "Yes, but what is the question?" After all, if question and answer are interrelated, asking the right question is crucial. What is the basic question to which Christ is the answer? What does the gospel reveal concerning the basic question of human existence? Well, I'm sure that it could be stated in different terms, but one way to state it is as follows: "How can persons be properly related to God, neighbor, world, and self?" From start to finish this is a question of relationships. Put this way, both the question of human need and the question of Christian conversion become relational questions. This is consistent with the theological position unfolded so far.

Stating the question of human need and God's response in relational categories keeps us from localizing sin in one specific aspect of human nature. Broken relationships cannot be defined that narrowly. But this way of stating the question does allow us to address the multi-dimensional nature of both sin and Christian conversion. It will also help us to come to grips with the centrifugal force of sin. Not only does sin separate us from our Creator, it also pulls us out of harmony with our neighbors, ourselves, as well as our whole environment. If salvation is to come, therefore, it will not come simply to independent unconnected individuals in isolation from one another and the world; it will come to whole persons in their whole world. Moreover, if human need is relational, then Christian conversion has to be more than mental assent to a list of propositions. And evangelism has to be more than clever slogans on bumper stickers; more than "spiritual laws" or propositions that we toss like rocks upon people's heads; more than handy-dandy gimmicks and spiked-up programs designed to get people to do what we want them to do. If the gospel reveals the basic question of human existence as a relational one, then the answer must be commensurate with the question—the answer must be relational as well. How does the gospel inform us regarding the relational needs of the human being and God's response to those needs?

Several of us working fulltime in the field of evangelism have advocated for several years now that evangelism should aim for the salvation of the total person. But, who is the person? In what sense are people in bondage to sin and what are the dimensions of that bondage? When we look carefully at contemporary Christian attempts to answer this question we discover that there are at least two distinct currents of thought which run side by side. One current holds that the person is a self-contained being who has relationships to other persons and to society, and these relationships are essentially external to the sinful self. It follows that the sinful self is sinful because sin is transmitted biologically. It is inbred. In other words, the self is not really shaped by relationships, but is strictly individualistic and separate. To quote Edward Schillebeeckx:

> Such Christians are then working with the concept of an abstract individual who in his free subjectivity is completely isolated from the objective form of society in which people live and from the power that prevails there. They forget how deeply and inwardly the individual is involved in society, above all how he or she is conditioned to the depths of their [sic] innermost being by a specific society, with the particular needs that it has created.[15]

The source of much of this understanding can be found in the ideas of Aristotle. Aristotle taught that the ground of individual human identity could be found in the person's rational capacity. In the post-reformation theological systems of Protestant orthodoxy, Aristotle's philosophical basis was appropriated and integrated into doctrinal formulations. This tended to give orthodoxy's concept of personal salvation a rationalistic and individualistic flavor not found in the New Testament.

In addition, part of this idea of human nature has its rootage in the categories of faculty psychology—another inheritance from the ancient Greeks. According to this understanding, the individual is a composite of distinct parts or faculties which operate as separate units. Once faculty psychology was appropriated by the church, it became necessary to draw sharp distinctions between the material body and the spiritual soul as two separate parts of each person's being. The spirit or soul was understood as a distinct, non-material, self-contained substance—a kind of spiritual form, living in the physical body and temporarily making use of it. Since this analysis of the human being was assumed to be commensurate with the psychology of the New Testament, it provided many of the categories for an individualistic view of sin and conversion. Fundamental to this view is that the soul is formed independently of social interaction. Primarily, the soul reveals itself in the activity of the mind (reason) rather than in social relationships. It follows that conversion is a matter of the soul's relationship to God. Therefore, in this view, it is the individual, autonomous, private soul which is saved, and conversion has nothing essentially to do with reconciliation to other human beings or reconciliation within the social fabric of the community. Moreover, conversion tends to be a matter of belief or giving assent to a list of doctrinal statements.

Arguments from creation were employed to buttress Aristotle's concept of the rational soul. The rational soul as the distinctive human faculty was equated with the biblical idea of the image of God in the human being. And, whereas the Bible speaks of the whole Adam being created in God's image, this perspective tended to think of the image as a particular aspect or faculty in Adam's composite being. Moreover, this interpretation assumed that "Adam" meant individual man (for some time the male sex) rather than humankind. Thus, according to this position, God breathed into each individual an immortal, rational soul, and it is that soul which is of infinite worth, not the total person.[16]

Those who adhere to this view assume that if you can save individualistic souls first, then these saved souls will change bad relationships and evil societal structures. I wish it were that simple, don't you? But it isn't that simple because this is a limited view of the nature of human beings. Why? Well, because the person doesn't just *have* relationships. It is impossible to separate me from that network of relationships that makes me who I am. My relationships fashion me even as I attempt to fashion my relationships. Therefore, if you really want to get to me—that is, to who I am as a person—then you must get at my relationships. If my relationships are all wrong then I am all wrong. The only person that I know is the relational person. As someone has said, "Every *I* is a *we!*" Every person is a plural. There is no "I" without "we." Each of us to a large degree is shaped by a social group. Therefore, to know one's self is to also understand one's "people." In this sense there is no psychology without sociology.

## PERSONS IN RELATIONSHIP

A serious look at the Bible will reveal that the individual is in fact a relational person. This is stated clearly in the creation stories. As we have observed, the individual was made for community, and the Bible envisions, as the goal of all creation, the human family living under God's vision of *shalom*. The generic use of Adam to depict both the individual and humankind is evidence of this. Actually, it is humankind that stands at the pinnacle of God's created process and not the perfected, rational, individual male of Aristotelian philosophy.

Moreover, a serious look at the creation accounts will reveal that human beings in the totality of their psychosocial selves were made in the image of God. This image is not a special rational-spiritual faculty breathed into the human being. When God breathed into us the breath of life, we became living whole beings (*nefesh*), and God looked at us in our totality and said, "Good!" Thus, Adam (humankind) is in God's image, and individuals express that image in their relationships. As Gene Tucker has said, "The human being . . . is not a three-part being such as body, mind, and soul. Nor even a combination of body and spirit, but body—natural, physical stuff represented as 'dust'—and life—represented by the 'breath' from God. The human being is an animated body, a wholeness which cannot really be separated." [17]

Finally, the biblical understanding of the image of God is associated with humankind's ability to hear and respond to the living God. The human being is "response-able." By God's grace the human can respond to God and the neighbor. Adam is the relational creature whose essence is social. As relational beings we are not only responsible to God but are responsible for our brothers and sisters and also responsible for the very earth upon which we stand. This biblical understanding of our nature is summed up beautifully by Norman Kraus: "To be a person in the Biblical sense is to be a subject, an 'I,' in relation with another subject, a 'thou,' under the convenant of God. A person is an individual-in-community. Not only is such a person a mind-body (psychosomatic) unity, but also a social-spiritual unity. Outside of authentic relationships in community, personhood is a mere capacity. Mature personhood is the gift of God in convenant community. In the New Testament language we speak of it as wholeness or maturity in Christ." [18]

Obviously, the biblical concept of conversion is closely associated with this understanding of personhood. For in order to redeem this person, that network of relationships must also be redeemed. This is why repentance is more than just individual remorse for "my" sins. It is that, but it is more than that, because my guilt cannot be restricted to personal sins only. My guilt must be seen as a participation in the sin and guilt of the whole world. Isaiah understood this and said, "I am a man of unclean lips, and I dwell in the midst of a people of unclean lips" (Isa. 6:5). Therefore, the biblical understanding of personhood helps us see that salvation must include social redemption. If I am the sum and substance of my relationships, Christian conversion cannot be restricted to that which transpires in my individual soul but must include the transformation of that network of relationships which makes me who I am. Anything else is less than what God envisions for his creation. But even this is not the whole picture.

There is another popular current of thought in today's world, the notion that salvation can be effected by social redemption alone. This position assumes that persons are essentially innocent victims of evil and oppressive social structures; if we can either change those evil structures or help the innocent person escape from their clutches, the person will be free and will blossom into a thing of beauty.

Now, no one is denying the fact that persons are victimized by oppressive structures and relationships. This is undeniably true. We grow up in a world and participate in societal structures that are not congenial to what we are meant for—love. Most societal structures are based on personal or collective self-interests. Therefore, greed, ambition, party interest, and competition abound and are only held in check by the realization that we cannot safeguard our own self-interests without giving some place for those of others.

Sin is, therefore, more than personal and interpersonal; it is also, in the words of Hendrikus Berkhof, "suprapersonal." He maintains that the personal and interpersonal dimensions are based on mutual influencing, but the suprapersonal is "based not so much on the mentality of persons as on the driving force inherent both in institutions of our established society and in the anonymous powers of current codes of behaviour, taboos, traditions or the dictates of fashion." [19] He suggests that all these dimensions hang together. "First, personal sin broadens itself, assuming an interpersonal shape, and then, continuing, it concentrates or institutionalizes itself in suprapersonal magnitudes." He equates the suprapersonal dimension of sin with what Paul called "principalities and powers." [20] In every age people are threatened by a number of powerful and enslaving ideologies and taskmasters. These forces undermine us and our communities and rob us of our dignity and creativity. In our day we see these "principalities and powers" expressed in racism, poverty, oppression of minority groups, exploitation, ruthless dictatorships to the right and to the left, militarism and materialism.

To live in this world is to take part in and fall victim to these fallen social orders, which for the most part, do not value us. It is no surprise, therefore, that we feel trapped in a labryrinth of demonic structures and cry out for liberation. But, suppose liberation comes. Is the person who is liberated from oppressive cultural restraints really an innocent person? Is his or her personhood already authentic and simply waiting to be fulfilled? Is the liberated person an intrinsically good person who is merely victimized by environment? What understanding is it which assumes that the removal of oppressive societal structures imposed by others will automatically free the person who is essentially innocent? This is not the Christian view of human nature. In the Christian view the matter is not that simple, and for two reasons.

First, as we have already seen, sin is more than social dysfunction. In the nineteenth century a liberal optimism flourished which taught that human nature was fundamentally good and that sin and evil were largely caused by ignorance and bad housing. The prescribed antidote for this malady was a program of education and housing reform aimed at enabling people to live together in happiness and good will. However, no matter how well meaning, this illusion was eventually shattered by the hard facts of history. Though educational opportunities spread rapidly (especially in the western world) and many welfare programs were developed, nevertheless, the atrocities which accompanied two world wars and subsequent international conflicts, the continuance of political oppression and racial discrimination, and the general increase of violence, crime, and sexual permissiveness have forced many people all over the world to admit the existence in every person of what the Bible calls sin.

Albert Outler contends: "If . . . sin is merely social dysfunction, then it ought in principle to be corrigible and salvation ought really to be possible by some formula or program of self-salvation or group salvation. And yet in the long history of social activism there is no evidence whatever that persons or groups or societies have ever achieved their full human potential by means of human wisdom or heroism or even 'letting be' (save on some relative scale of amelioration that always falls short of our proper human hunger for the utmost). Nor is there any credible prospect for it, apart from the euphoric visions of our currently fashionable 'human potential' optimists." [21] The tragic element of life goes deeper than social dysfunction. Therefore, a mere program of education, though helpful in its own right, will not root out evil and injustice.

William Temple's definition of sin supports this point: "I am the centre of the world I see; where the horizon is depends on where I stand. . . . Education may make my self-centeredness less disastrous by widening my horizon of interest; so far it is like climbing a tower, which widens the horizon for physical vision, while leaving me still the centre and standard of reference." [22]

Second, salvation cannot be accomplished by social redemption alone because we are always guilty accomplices in our bondage, even when we are "the sinned against." We are both sinner and sinned against.[23] But, the nature of sin is such that we tend to refuse any personal responsibility for it. Therefore, we stress the miserable condition of our environment to the degree that it becomes a cowardly excuse for sin! We often take refuge in such things as the demonic power of structures or environmental factors, with the result that we excuse ourselves from responsibility. The Christian faith, however, walks a tight wire between human helplessness and responsibility, and we dare not do less. We may lament, "If I had not been born into that environment and conditioned by it, I would not have become such a person." But the scriptures teach that even in a paradise such as Eden humankind refused to allow the living God to be the center of life. Each human being, not of necessity but inevitably, repeats that performance. Sin is more than the result of our conditioning; it is also the cause. For anyone who believes in the living God, any sociopolitical liberation is only partial; indeed, if it claims to be *total*, it essentially becomes a new form of servitude or bondage.

So the Christian faith calls into question the assertion that human beings are essentially innocent and good. To say that we do sinful things solely because we are enmeshed in evil structures is a romantic view of human nature. Isaiah did not "cop out" by saying, "I am a man of unclean lips *because* I dwell in the midst of a people of unclean lips." No! He had the integrity to claim solidarity with his world. He knew that you cannot separate the guilty self from society anymore than you can separate the guilty society from the self.[24]

The Apostle Paul understood the person as a psychosomatic unity. As such, sin cannot be restricted either to the body, the soul, or the environment. All are implicated if the self is a unity. Human beings are indivisibly *whole* and the salvation of the gospel is likewise whole, pertaining here and now to the totality of human life and not only to part of it. Christian conversion, therefore, must mean the rectification of the total person and in relationship to body, others, and God. For Paul, the idea of an autonomous self is an illusion. Moreover, he would think it equally illusory to imagine that simply repealing repressive structures and social evils would bring salvation. Because of the nature of the self, the whole self is implicated in the human dilemma. So, taking away repressive external structures would not leave an innocent self ready to flourish but a distorted self needing conversion. The problem of evil is not located in society alone; it is also located in the human being.

In summary, the scriptures give us a "balanced" view of sin. Sin is not only a contagious disease; it is a cumulative process related to the social and cosmic dimensions of the world. It not only pollutes us, it pollutes the air we breathe and becomes incarnate in the very structures of human life and society. It is multidimensional. John Westerhoff supports this balanced view. He says, "The isolated individual self is a fiction but so is the social self. To affirm only a social self is to over-emphasize the role nurture and socialization play in framing us. To affirm only the individual self, naked and responsible before God, is to underestimate the significance of other historical actors in our lives. In truth we are corporate selves who live in a continual dynamic relationship with all others and with God. The self is constituted by its relationships; human life is essentially corporate." [25]

Any theology of Christian conversion worth its salt must deal with all the deep and tragic dimensions in human nature, human relations, and social structures. Moreover, as we recognize that sin is much more than a private concern, we will regain the full, personal, social, and cosmic meaning of Christian conversion. If sin has a structural and cosmic effect, salvation must also have a structural and cosmic dimension. Not only does the human heart need changing but so do social, economic, and cultural structures as well.

Who or what could possibly deliver us from this tragedy called sin without robbing us of our freedom and thus also of our full humanity?

## QUESTIONS FOR THOUGHT AND DISCUSSION

1. A major premise of this chapter is that "our human condition" is most truly and fully exposed by God's revelation through the gospel. What are the values and weaknesses of this assumption?

2. What meanings, feelings, and memories does the word *sin* call up in you? How would you summarize the author's understanding of sin? Your own?

3. Try phrasing ten or more questions for which "Christ is the answer" (p. 88), that is, for which Christian conversion is the needed response.

4. A strong case is made for the fact that sin is relational and that neither individual change nor social change alone is an adequate solution. Describe a sinful social system in which you take part, and how you and it affect each other. What sort of conversion is required?

# 7. CHRISTIAN CONVERSION: FACETS OF THE PROCESS

## Part One

Earlier we acknowledged that Christian conversion happens when the gospel is communicated and responded to, that the music of Christian conversion comes from strings drawn taut between two points: divine initiative and human response. This is in keeping with the central focus of Wesley's theology: the saving work of Christ and the human appropriation of that work.[1] The primary emphasis of earlier chapters has been upon divine initiative. Now, we must turn to the human side of Christian conversion. What does it mean to respond affirmatively to the gospel? What are the contours of that response?

Please be aware that in this chapter and the next the sequence in which the various dimensions of conversion appear is quite arbitrary. This caution must be highlighted because of our tendency to take one specific order or model of conversion and stereotype it as valid for all persons. This tendency must be avoided because it does an injustice to the scriptures and to human beings. Christian conversion happens to different persons in different ways, at different stages of life, and on different levels. To stereotype a certain order as the "only way" constitutes a serious perversion of the biblical perspective and puts a tragic limitation on the scope of the gospel's power. More will be said about this issue in the following chapters. Here, it will be my purpose to present Christian conversion as a dynamic process that involves some combination of the following elements.

## CHRISTIAN CONVERSION MEANS DISCOVERING
## THE POSSIBILITY OF A NEW FOCUS

Suppose persons come to a realization that they are out of focus. Suppose they realize that something is fundamentally wrong with their whole life but they feel powerless to help themselves. Suppose they see themselves as sated with precepts but longing for power—what they ought to do they cannot do. Suppose they realize with Isaiah that they are persons "of unclean lips . . . in the midst of a people of unclean lips . . ." (Isaiah 6:5), sensing both their own sin and their solidarity with other sinners. Suppose they see themselves and their neighbors as imprisoned by principalities and powers that are so immense that they seem uncontrollable. Suppose they see their future as being somehow inevitably determined by historical movements and forces and feel that they are walking a tightwire between human helplessness and responsibility. What then? What is the answer to Paul's poignant question: "Miserable creature that I am, who is there to rescue me out of this body doomed to death?" (Rom. 7:24-25).

Some say there is no answer. They contend that the human condition and the human situation are irrevocably set. Human nature and social structures cannot be changed. Sin is not only serious; it is invincible. People are hopelessly lost and can only go from bad to worse. Examples of this pessimistic attitude are plentiful.

First, there are those who meet the prospect of creative change with cynicism. Voltaire once quoted a saying that goes something like this: "The better I get to know people, the better I like dogs." Does this not reflect the feeling of many people in today's world? I am amazed at the cynicism that lurks barely beneath the surface of our facade of optimism. One college student said to me, "The church says that God wants to save people, but maybe people aren't worth saving!" According to the cynic, truth and goodness are completely beyond the experience of the human being.

Others would say that the possibility of creative change is nullified by determinism. People cannot experience change because they are subject to antecedents and previous conditions that hold them in bondage. In describing this determinism the late president of The World Methodist Council, Bishop F. Gerald Ensley, delineated two categories: rigid and flexible. The more rigid type teaches that human life is the result of forces operating from without. These controlling forces may be natural laws, the fixed patterns of psychological existence, vast economic or social complexes, or (for the more speculative) cosmic processes such as fate or deity. On the other hand, the more flexible type of determinism assumes that life is not determined from without but from within. Thus people do what they do because of their inner nature, and to assume that they can do otherwise is an illusion.[2]

Bishop Ensley concludes that determinism is much more effective in dealing with nonhuman entities than persons. He admits that natural science has had great success with its assumption that events in the space-time world are bound in an unvarying causal link. The trouble comes when people are treated as though they were cause-and-effect mechanisms and nothing more. Ensley says, "Determinism is not convincing as an explanation of success. When a man is venal, vindictive, or cruel we may say, 'That's human nature.' But when a person rises to the heights of saintliness, artistic creativity, or intellectual achievement, we rarely hear reference to its necessity. We instinctively recognize that something more than heredity, environment, or chance has entered in." He concludes, "The truth is that determinism is a gross oversimplification of life. It covers everything with a verbal blanket: 'All is determined.' But while such determinism is productive in enabling us to predict happenings in nature, it is a washout in forecasting human history."[3]

Still others would give religious reasons for denying the possibility of creative change. The writer of Ecclesiastes was a fascinating poet but a gloomy and pessimistic preacher! He says a number of things that make him sound very much like the modern skeptic. In one place he laments, "That which is crooked cannot be made straight" (Eccl. 1:15). Few things are more devastating to the human spirit and the human community than the quiet acquiescence which allows us to accept the inevitability of sin and injustice. It is this attitude which encourages the militarist to say war is "inevitable," or the modern person involved in business to say, "It is necessary to compromise principle in order to get ahead in this world," or the callous person to say, "Filthy prisons and death are all that criminals deserve."

Moreover, this same attitude is seen in a number of us who attend church every week. We regularly pray that we may ever hereafter "serve and please God in newness of life," or that we may hereafter live "a godly, righteous, and sober life," only to leave the place of worship remaining basically irritable, selfish, unwilling to serve, caught in the same old habits and defiant of every suggestion regarding change. Many of us become duped into believing that creative change is impossible. We tend to accept evils and wrongs as inevitable and give up the fight. This "sloth" encourages us to acquiesce to sin and injustice in ourselves and in our world. Therefore, in the words of Jeremiah, "No one repents of his wickedness saying: What have I done? . . . People do not know the ruling of Yahweh! They feel no shame, they have forgotten how to blush" (Jer. 8:5-7, 12). We become so accustomed to doing wrong that we assume we cannot do right. With Jeremiah we ask, "Can the Ethiopian change his skin, or the leopard his spots?" (Jer. 13:23). We assume that things can only go from bad to worse. Any religion of futility that considers people to be helpless, ineffectual pawns, determined and without self-determination, powerless to initiate, to interrupt, or to alter causative sequences must be examined with an eye to finding out whether this is not one more subtle attempt to avoid human responsibility and commitment.

Sometimes elaborate doctrinal systems, which deny the possibilities of creative change, are dogmatically held. One such doctrine is the Calvinist doctrine of total depravity. When this doctrine is pushed to the limit it becomes what Albert Outler calls "tee-total depravity." In actuality one sees very little difference between this doctrine and that worked out by the Roman Stoic, Seneca. Seneca also developed a radical doctrine of total depravity. He once said, "Not only have we done wrong, but we shall go on doing wrong to the very end of life." Again he said, "Wicked we are, wicked we have been, and, I regret to add, wicked we always will be." [4] Some push the doctrine of total depravity to the point that people are even anaesthetized against remorse, regret, and repentance.

I am inclined to believe that the doctrine of "tee-total depravity" is itself a result of the radical nature of sin, for it causes us to suppose that we are hopelessly lost. Albert Outler points out that the radical nature of sin is such that it not only causes people to suppose they can save themselves (which is false), but it also causes people to suppose they are hopelessly lost (which is equally false). In support of this Outler claims that the "gist of sin is man's false perception of God's wrath, or of his mercy, or of his absence." [5]

Wesley refused to accept the Calvinist view of "tee-total depravity." He believed in original sin, but as we have seen, it is a malignant disease rather than the actual destruction of the image of God in the sinner. He believed in total depravity but understood it to mean that the entire person and not just a part is affected by sin. Yet he avoided the Lutheran view of humankind as invincibly concupiscent and the Calvinist assumption regarding the human being's fated idolatry. He wanted to hold to the person's divinely created free will, "limited but real—corrupted and perverted by sin but never cancelled." [6] According to Wesleyan theology, "human life is meaningfully related to God even in sin and estrangement; the sinner has some dim, imperfect knowledge of God in his fleeting moments of transcendental or mystical awareness; his moral conscience is deadened but not destroyed." [7]

It is false, therefore, to suppose that human beings are hopelessly lost. Sin is serious but not invincible! Our situation is never so good that we are not the potential victims of sin both working in us and on us, and our situation is never so bad that there are not possibilities of new life and redemption. No matter how warped and twisted the nature of the human being, the Christian faith insists that something beautiful can blossom in the sunshine of God's love. Because of God's sovereign power nothing is irrevocably set. Nothing is so twisted, so tired, so wrong, or so hopeless that it cannot be "born again" into new life. No matter how serious the nature of sin, no matter how broken and confused the human situation, no matter how many years people and communities have sat in their dull and lifeless insensitivity, God can "make all things new."

Thus a part of the new focus in Christian conversion is the dawning possibility that human nature and society can be changed for the better. They can go from bad to good. Now this Christian view is no shallow optimism concerning human nature, nor is it an idealistic utopianism in terms of our future history. The Christian faith is pessimistic and freed from illusion about our possibilities apart from God. But the Christian faith is very optimistic and filled with hope about our possibilities, life's meaning, and the world's future when properly related to God.[8]

In Christian faith we find the very reverse of the cynicism, pessimism, and determinism which insist we must simply accept the grim fact that we are irremediably and irredeemably evil. Christian faith is committed to a dynamic which proclaims that persons need not stay the way they are. Theirs need not be an existence of invincible concupiscence or fated idolatry. There is a positive answer to Paul's question (Rom. 7:24-25) precisely because it is the right question. Paul's ability to put the question so poignantly comes as a result of God's work in his life. Moreover, it is because Paul knows the *Answer* that he puts the question in such poignant terms. His is the Christian way of putting the question of human existence. It is evoked by a conscience sensitized by the Spirit of the living God. Therefore, when Paul asks, "Who will deliver me?" the answer comes back: "God alone, through Jesus Christ our Lord! Thanks be to God!" (Rom. 7:24-25). That *is* the answer! Only God can bring a person's life into focus. What nothing or no one else could do for us, "God has done: by sending his Son" (Rom. 8:3).

Thus, preliminary to, and yet concurrent with, the conversion process is the dawning discovery that life might possibly have a new focus. Persons, situations, and structures can be changed. It is possible for a sour person to become sweet, a proud person humble, and a selfish person generous. Even powerful societal structures can become more humanizing and just. These miracles can and do happen. They are a part of the glory of the gospel. The revelation of God in Jesus Christ is powerful enough to change not only our standing before God but our very nature. It not only has the power to redeem persons but also includes a witness that remodels the world. As we have seen, that's what Christian conversion is about. It literally means a change of direction, a wheeling about, a U-turn in life.

Our study of the biblical words for Christian conversion caused us to conclude that conversion depicts a profound change in the sinner, a facing in a new direction; in short, deep and genuine change. A transforming encounter with the living God results in a change or reorientation in all our relationships, including relationships to the world, to possessions, to the poor and dispossessed, to violence in society, to the idols of culture, and to the false worship of the state.

Christian conversion, therefore, is more than a sentimental or aesthetic experience which lasts for an hour or two and then disappears. Neither is it a philosophy of life accepted for a time as a working hypothesis, a beneficent illusion which we persuade ourselves to believe because of the comfort or social benefit we hope it will bring. Christian conversion means radical life-change. It controls our relationship to everything that we regard as life's reality, so that if reality be anywhere it must be in conversion. Christian conversion is more than a novel transitory experience, it is a transformation. It is not enough to say we have changed. More precisely, we *are* changed, and changed in a decisive way.

Moreover, the changes that result from Christian conversion are real, not illusory. The experience of Christian conversion can be integrated into life in a way which is impossible with dreams or illusions. We recognize a dream as a dream, not because it is not vivid, for it may be intensely so, but because it cannot be worked into the whole fabric of life. As P. T. Forsyth put it, "If we sail through the air on a broomstick at two in the morning, or inherit a legacy of millions at five, we cannot safely work the experience into the day's outlook or the day's conduct. . . . The test of a dream is not to pinch one's self, to get over one vivid impression by another. . . . The test is practice. The dream does not work, meaning by that not that it does not succeed, but that it is not in the context of our moral life. Such is all hallucination. But reality is in organic connection with life's whole." [9]

Christian conversion is in such organic connection. It not only places us in communion with God, it puts us in step with the whole moral order which had previously been against us. What we cannot do with dreams of flying broomsticks or legacies we can do with our experience of Christian conversion. It can be treated as real and we can live our lives in terms of it because it means genuine change, not illusion.

For many people the experience of vulnerability is the beginning of the human response in conversion. Many people come by the discovery of the possibility of Christian conversion via the avenue of remorse, discontent, despair, uneasiness or grief over the shallowness, meaninglessness or emptiness of their lives. A number of contemporary scholars confirm this observation. Albert Outler contends that the person who finally hears God's good news is usually the one who, beforehand, "was either desperate or empty." [10] Thus a young woman writes: "It was in my darkest hour, in the moment of deepest despair, that faith began to well up in me like a bubbling spring. In the midst of my greatest awareness of the tragedy of the human condition, the inevitability of human sin, I began miraculously to hope."

Many times this vulnerability thrusts itself upon persons during crisis situations, conflicts, or what Charles Gerkin calls extreme or boundary situations, "in which the fundamental contradictions between human aspirations and finite possibilities become visible in such a way as to demand attention." [11] In a similar vein Wayne Oates states the issue of vulnerability in terms of conflict. He says there must be some conflict between the self that I am and the self I want to become, the life that is and the better life that can be. The resolution of this conflict is the essence of the conversion experience. In this view, "if there is no conflict, there is not likely to be any conversion." [12] In like manner Paul Johnson insists that "unless a person is aware of conflict serious enough to defeat him, and unless he is concerned ultimately to put his life in the balance, he is not ready for conversion." [13]

In an illuminating study of Christian conversion Jacques Pasquier, the Roman Catholic scholar, observes the same phenomenon:

> One comes into touch with one's own powerlessness and sinfulness. We come into touch with our finitude and limitedness or brokenness. I think it is when we come to this point that, in the experience of *helplessness*, we begin to realize that running from place to place, knocking on all the doors, is leading us nowhere. . . . In the experience of silence, the Word begins to speak to us. In the experience of darkness, the light begins to shine: very uncertain, very weak, yet becoming more and more real. What is left is . . . an emptiness, a vulnerability which is the beginning of conversion.[14]

Their observation of this same process led Holmes and Westerhoff to depict conversion as a movement from orientation, to disorientation, to reorientation. Conversion is more than the discovery of an assurance we did not have before. The nonbeliever is often quite comfortable and self-assured even though the source of that comfort and assurance is a form of tranquilization. People tend to become content with their life of sin. Thus, the onset of Christian conversion is characterized by *disorientation* as all our false assurances and comforts are subverted and we are led to "the edge of the abyss of the unknown and uncontrollable." [15]

But Christian conversion is possible only if, at the time we experience disorientation, we can see alternatives or at least the possibility of reorientation. If the human being reaches a crisis point and there are no redemptive alternatives then he or she is led to depression, and sometimes, to suicide. Not only must there be a realization of the need for profound change; there must also be at least a glimmer of hope that help is available to accomplish that change. There must be some awareness that there is something "out there" to respond to. After studying a number of Christian conversions, Keith Miller discovered that in practically every case there was not only a dawning awareness of something "beyond" but a common feeling of being drawn toward a "presence" while simultaneously having faced the shock of vulnerability.[16]

To summarize, we have said that God's action in Christ makes it possible for persons, situations, and structures to be changed. There is hope, hope that even this death-centered world can be focused. There is hope that the greedy can become generous; the jealous, magnanimous; the arrogant, humble; the mean, kindly. There is hope that human triviality can be overcome as people come to grips with fundamental reality. There is hope that the aimless, indolent, and idle can come alive to a new purpose. There is hope that the bored and cynical can find joy. There is hope that sinful structures which dehumanize and degrade can be brought in line with God's vision of a new world order.

In other words, there is hope that human lives, relationships, and structures, though blurred by sin, can be focused. It is God who puts these glimmers of hope within us, helping us to see that there might possibly be a new beginning. Moreover, it is in and through this dawning discovery of a new possibility, that God is preparing our lives for confrontation with a new and vital dynamic.

## CONVERSION MEANS CONFRONTING A SAVING DYNAMIC

We have seen how Christian conversion happens on God's terms, at God's initiative, and in accordance with God's grace, and how God has made saving grace known in the good news of salvation (Chapter 4). Thus we have learned that the motivating dynamic in Christian conversion is always the grace of God made known to us through Jesus Christ. Salvation is by grace and grace alone (Acts 20:24; Rom. 4:16; 1 Cor. 15:10).

*Grace* is the term we use to speak of God's initiative, God's going-before or "prevenience." Grace means the benevolent and merciful (and at the same time free and sovereign) love of God for people. As we have seen, this grace is witnessed in the very nature of God but it primarily manifests itself in the action of God in history—especially in the birth, life, death, and resurrection of

Jesus Christ. Thus grace provides a new dynamic for redemption, liberation, and renewal of life. It is this unmerited grace of God revealed in and through the deeds of God (Chapter 4) which provides the saving dynamic in Christian conversion.

The New Testament not only stresses the fact that God's grace is an unconditional free gift, it also highlights its abundance (Rom. 5:15, 20; 6:1; 2 Cor. 9:8,14). The all-embracing sign of the abundance of God's grace is Jesus' suffering and death on the cross (Rom. 5:9-11; 1 Cor. 15:2f). "If God is on our side," said Paul, "who is against us? He did not spare his own Son, but gave Him up for us all; with this gift how can he fail to lavish upon us all he has to give" (Rom. 8:31-32)? So the cross is more than the supreme illustration of the sinfulness of people; it is the concrete expression of the suffering love of God declaring the conviction that we are loved perfectly, ultimately, and seriously by God.

A large part of the mystery of Christian conversion is related to the incomprehensibility of God's grace. There is no explanation for it. Certainly, the "love of God *is* greater far than tongue or pen could ever tell." Like countless others I can only add my voice to that of Paul and say, "Oh the depth of the riches and the wisdom and the knowledge of God! How his decisions are beyond the mind of man to trace! How mysterious are his ways! For who has known the mind of the Lord?" (Rom. 11:33-34, Barclay's translation). Even if we spent an eternity we could never fathom the unceasing wonder of the inexpressible grace of God. It is "amazing"! God's grace confronts us with a generosity so overwhelming that any thought of earning or deserving that grace or presenting a claim on God is completely out of place.

Therefore, to experience the grace of God in Christ is to have one's religious ideas completely transformed and reinterpreted. Once we have experienced grace, there can be no more talk of human merit. Like Paul, we find ourselves exulting over the "free gift of grace," "grace reigning," "grace abounding through Christ," or "the sphere of grace in which we stand." We find our lives being dominated by the reality of divine grace manifested in Christ (Rom. 5).

Grace teaches us that discipleship no longer needs to flow forth from the hard, distant, and exacting righteousness of God which simply imposes commands and duties and watches for disobedience with a penalizing eye, encouraging people to obey for fear of consequences or out of hope of reward. Jonathan Edwards paints a graphic picture which depicts the plight of those who attempt to subvert the grace of God by trusting in their own abilities and endeavors:

> They set themselves upon a new course of fruitless endeavors in their own strength to make themselves better, and still meet with new disappointments: they are earnest to inquire what they should do. . . . It may be they hope they are something better than they were; but then the pleasing dream all vanishes again. If they are told that they trust too much to their own strength and righteousness, they cannot unlearn this practice all at once, and find not yet the appearance of any good, but all looks as dark as midnight. Thus they wander about from mountain to hill, seeking rest and finding none: when they are beat out of one refuge they fly to another.[17]

We humans have a difficult time learning that we cannot earn God's grace. But we do not have to! It is the abundant gift of God for salvation (Eph. 2:5). Because of Christ, we are lifted out of a religion of works righteousness and into a new experience of reconciliation to God. Now obedience is no longer a matter of drudgery or compliance in order to get rewards, but rather a matter of gratitude for God's grace.

It is helpful to see this process in terms of Wesleyan theology. Here we learn that even in our sin God puts within us the ability to face up to our deep need, to recognize that we could be more than we are, to know that we cannot save ourselves, and to believe help is available. Though we are out of focus, God's grace helps us know that genuine focus is possible. John Wesley called this gift prevenient (or preventing) grace, that is, grace that "goes before." In Wesley's view, grace was understood and experienced as dynamic influence, or as Outler puts it, "God's love, immanent and active in human life." Moreover, grace is "prior initiative" which makes "every human action a reaction; hence, it is 'preventing.'"[18]

So, in Wesleyan terms,

> Salvation begins with what is usually termed (and very properly) preventing grace; including the first wish to please God, the first dawn of light concerning His will, and the first light transient conviction having sinned against Him. All these imply some tendency toward life; some degree of salvation; the beginning of a deliverance from a blind unfeeling heart, quite insensible of God and the things of God.[19]

Again, in his sermon on "The Fullness of Faith," Wesley defines prevenient grace as "all the drawings of the Father; the desires after God which, if we yield to them increase more and more; all that 'light' wherewith the Son of God 'enlighteneth everyone that cometh into the world' (c.f. John 1:9), showing every man 'to do justly, to love mercy, and to walk humbly with his God' (c.f. Micah 6:8); all the 'convictions' which His spirit, from time to time, works in every child of man.'"[20] In another sermon Wesley tells how preventing grace comes through to people:

> Therefore, at such times as he seeth good, [God] gives a dawning of light unto them that sit in darkness. He causes a part of his good news to pass before them, and shows that he is a God that heareth the prayer. They see the promise, which is by faith in Christ Jesus, though it be yet afar off; and hereby they are encouraged to "run with patience the race which is set before them."[21]

Prevenient grace teaches us that many people are in dialogue with God without being aware of it. Sometimes this happens because their values are called into question and they enter into a terrible inner struggle. Sometimes it happens when a person asks deep questions about the world, about the meaning of things, about the meaning of disease and healing, life and death. Paul Tillich contends that the asking of deep questions with genuine seriousness is a sign that God is already at work in a person's life. He says, "He who is ultimately concerned about his place of estrangement and about the possibility of reunion with the ground and aim of his being is already in the grip of the Spiritual Presence." [22]

Sometimes this happens when a person becomes conscious of weakness or of responsibility or of shortcomings and asks if there is any way out. It is God who puts these questions to us and within us. It is God who is speaking through the power of the Holy Spirit even though we may not realize it. People have witnessed to this on countless occasions when they testify that nothing that went before their conversion to Christ was meaningless. Everything, including their earlier hesitations and rebellions and wanderings and protests against Christ, was part of the pattern. But they did not know this at the time.[23]

John Wesley taught that this prevenient grace of God working through the conscience is the beginning of the conversion process. This grace is universally available, "free for all and in all." But prevenient grace working through the conscience is not enough. Further gifts are necessary to enable a person to come to Christian conversion. Therefore, God is made known not only through prevenient grace, but also, and more decisively, in the gospel. It is the gospel that reveals God's justifying grace. Jesus "was delivered up for our trespasses and was raised for our justification" (Rom. 4:25, RSV). If the person responds affirmatively to prevenient grace (and there is always freedom to respond affirmatively or negatively) that response eventuates in a further gift, justifying grace. Wesley says, "Stir up the spark of grace which is now in you and [God] will give you more grace." [24]

Wesley understood justification as pardon. He said, "The plain Scriptural notion of justification is pardon—the forgiveness of sins. It is that act of God the Father, whereby, for the sake of the propitiation made by the blood of his Son, He 'showeth forth his righteousness [mercy] by the remission of the sins that are past'" (Rom. 3:25). Wesley makes it clear that "forgiveness . . . has an immediate reference to sin, and, in this respect, to nothing else. It is our unrighteousness to which the pardoning God is merciful. It is our iniquity which He remembereth no more." [25] Again he says, "Justification is another word for pardon. It is the forgiveness of all our sins and, what is necessarily implied therein, our acceptance with God." [26]

The scriptures clearly teach that God *justifies* the ungodly. The word *justify* has several meanings. In common usage it can mean giving reasons or excuses, as when we say, "He is trying to justify himself." This is *not* the scriptural meaning of the word. When God justifies the ungodly, God is not giving excuses for their ungodliness.

In simplest form the word means "to make just." But even this definition tends to get in the way of the truth, because we tend to think of justice as being fair and equitable. To understand Paul's use of the word it is necessary to get behind the Greek to the Hebrew. In the Old Testament righteousness means "rightness" or the appropriate relationship to the norm. The verb *to make right*, therefore, does not mean "make just" but to "make the relationship right," to align. When God, therefore, justifies, right relationships are restored. Thus justification means the rectification of the relationships. When Paul says God is the "one who justifies the ungodly" (Rom. 4:5, RSV), he means God is the one who rectifies the ungodly, rectifies the relationship between the ungodly and the Creator and makes reconciliation possible. Moreover, from a righted relationship there comes a righted life. Indeed, a right life can only come from a right relationship to God.

Theodore Runyon gives the following summary of this good news of justification. It is:

. . . the new foundation laid by God in Christ Jesus, who is the outworking of the Father's redemptive intervention to release humanity from bondage. The Son does the Father's work in the world; he is the self-expression of the divine heart. His work alone provides the basis for reconciliation; it eliminates all human efforts toward self-justification because it makes them unnecessary. The new basis for relationship is his love which "has been poured into our hearts through the Holy Spirit which has been given to us." The reception of this love overcomes estrangement and is marked by the sense of forgiveness and liberation.[27]

So the motivating dynamic in Christian conversion is the gracious good news that God was and is in Jesus Christ reconciling the "whole universe unto Himself, making peace through the shedding of His blood upon the cross—to reconcile all things, whether on earth or in heaven through him alone" (Col. 1:20). The core of this saving dynamic is Jesus Christ, "the man of God's own choosing." His birth, life, death, and resurrection are active proof of God's love toward us (Rom. 5:8).

This decisive action of God in Christ has proclaimed and continues to proclaim to the whole world: You are pardoned, forgiven, accepted—NOW! Jesus taught that God's forgiveness is freely available in the "now" (Mark 2:1-12). He announced that God has already forgiven and acted decisively to prove it. In other words, forgiveness is past tense! Our sins are forgiven (1 John 2:12). Our trespasses are not counted against us (2 Cor. 5:19). This is why repentance and faith have become a possibility (Rom. 2:4). Without the dynamic of prevenient and justifying grace we could not repent or believe.

It is confrontation with this good news of God's grace which is the prelude for finding a whole new direction for life. God's forgiving love, God's grace, evokes radical change and unbinds us from the power of sin. The good news of God's accepting love takes the inevitability out of our history. We know that the power is now available for a new beginning, a new life. We can be liberated from everything that makes us less than what God intends us to be. Moreover, we begin to respond to the dawning realization that God is not only capable of focusing our personal lives, but God is actually ushering in a whole new order of things: a new humanity, a new heaven and a new earth, a new kingdom. Thus, the grace of God is as personal as our deepest human need and more powerful than the most resistant institutional or political structure.

This divine grace is made operative in our lives by the power of the Holy Spirit. The Holy Spirit is "God present as power with people." [28] The Holy Spirit convicts us of sin, shows us new possibilities, awakens faith, and prepares the heart, the mind, and the will to receive God's accepting grace. In this sense the presence of the Holy Spirit is the irreducible minimum in Christian conversion. Without the Holy Spirit nobody comes to trust the gospel or to live in terms of it. Therefore, even repentance and faith, which are clearly human responses, are, nevertheless, gifts of God (Acts 11:18; Eph. 2:8; Phil. 1:29). Paul says that no one confesses Jesus as Lord without the enabling power of the Spirit (1 Cor. 12:1-3). It is the Spirit that enables us to believe that through Jesus we are sons and daughters, heirs of God (Rom. 8:14-17).

So it is the Holy Spirit that opens our eyes to the grace that liberates us from bondage and brings us out of death into life. Through the power of the Holy Spirit we are enabled to pray (Rom. 8:26-27). We cannot produce faith and commitment by ourselves. We are dependent on the power of the Holy Spirit. For this reason Charles Wesley wrote: "Spirit of faith, come down,/Reveal the things of God;/. . . . No man can truly say/That Jesus is the Lord,/Unless thou take the veil away,/And breathe the living Word." [29] The Holy Spirit breaks down barriers, builds bridges and enables persons to respond to grace. The Holy Spirit makes us aware and sensitive to our own deep need and opens our lives to the powerful entrance of the gospel, evoking faith, kindling love, and illuminating the mighty acts of God.

In short, Christian conversion is a *response* to grace. But what is the nature of the human response to God's actions?

## QUESTIONS FOR THOUGHT AND DISCUSSION

1. This chapter describes several causes of our not believing in the possibility of human change: cynicism, determinism, a quiet acquiescence, the doctrine of depravity. . . . What others would you add?

2. Two factors that often occur early in the conversion experience are "the dawning discovery that life might possibly have a

new focus" (p. 103) and "the experience of vulnerability" (p. 105). In what ways has this been true in your own Christian life? In that of others you know?

3. Do you ever find yourself and others trying to "earn" God's love? Through what specific behaviors?

4. Amazing grace! List a hundred ways you have experienced God's unconditional free gift of love! Include examples of prevenient grace (ongoing love, drawing you toward God) and justifying grace (forgiving love).

5. Describe in your own words the way God's grace functions in our conversion.

# 8. Christian Conversion: Facets of the Process

## Part Two

### CHRISTIAN CONVERSION MEANS FAITH AND REPENTANCE

When we say yes to God's action in Christ, that is, when we respond in trust and commitment to this saving dynamic, things begin to happen! God begins to focus our lives. "Self-righteousness is displaced by the righteousness of Christ. By faith—and by faith alone!—uptight lives are relaxed, trapped lives liberated, arrogant lives humbled, soiled lives cleansed, slouching lives raised up to tiptoe, empty lives filled, life unto death turned into life unto life." [1] But what is the nature of this *faith* by which our lives are brought into focus?

Christian faith is a centered, personal, and relational act of trust and commitment.[2] It is centered in Jesus Christ. It results in a right relationship with God, the neighbor, one's self, and the world. It is a freely chosen personal relationship of trust and fidelity.

This Christian understanding of faith is being undermined today by a number of popular reductionisms. The first tends to reduce faith to belief, and belief to a set of doctrinal propositions. This robs faith of its personal-relational nature and binds people to impersonal dogma. It takes from faith the element of Abrahamic risk that encourages us to follow God into the unknown. It assumes that everything must be crystal clear, in black and white, or else faith is impossible. Any doubt is considered totally incompatible because propositional belief cannot tolerate any deviation from the stated dogma. This is an ideal system for those who wish to "park their intellect" and let someone else do their thinking for them. People tend to get "backed" into this reductionism because of heavy use of the words *believe* and *belief* to denote faith. This is because "faith" has no verb form. We cannot say, for instance, "She faiths." Therefore, we say, "She believes." This creates difficulty because the noun form "belief," does not mean the same thing as "faith." Nevertheless, because "believe" is associated with "belief," people assume that faith is "believing beliefs."

This is the root of the sort of propositional faith that John Wesley called "a dead faith." It is dead not because it fails to believe, but because its object is a set of opinions and notions rather than the living God. In two illuminating passages Wesley spells this out. First he defines "a dead faith" as follows:

> This faith is a persuasion that there is a God and a belief (of all the truths contained in His Word); so that it consisteth only in believing that the Word of God is true. And this is not properly called faith. But as he that readeth Caesar's *Commentary,* (though he believeth it) to be true, yet (he) is not properly said (to believe) in Caesar; even so he that believeth all the Bible (to be true) and yet liveth ungodly is not properly said (to believe) in God.[3]

Then Wesley points out the difference between "opinion" (what I have preferred to call "proposition") and genuine Christian faith. Notice how he highlights the personal-relational nature of faith:

> But what is faith? Not an opinion, no more than it is a form of words; not any number of opinions put together, be they ever so true. A string of opinions is no more Christian faith than a string of beads is Christian holiness. It is not an assent to any opinion, or any number of opinions. A man may assent to three or three and twenty creeds; he may assent to all the Old and New Testament (at least, as far as he understands them) and yet have no Christian faith at all. . . . Christian faith . . . in its

more particular notion, . . . is a divine evidence or conviction wrought in my heart that God is reconciled to *me* through his Son, inseparably joined with a confidence in Him as a gracious, reconciled Father.[4]

Again, Wesley says, "We are saved from our sins only by a confidence in the love of God. As soon as we 'behold what manner of love it is which the Father hath bestowed upon us (1 John 3:10), we love Him' (as the apostle observes) 'because he first loved us' (1 John 4:19)." [5] Now, as I have insisted, there is a content to faith. Faith does have an object. However, that content is a personal act of trust and commitment to that which the gospel announces, and not mental assent to propositions or opinions.

Another popular reductionism in the Western world is the trend toward "faith in faith." It operates out of the popular notion that it does not matter what a person believes so long as that person believes sincerely enough and fervently enough that it works. Faith is reduced to a psychological state and people are admonished to believe in faith. Paul Scherer characterizes this notion when he says, "It adds up to something like this: Have faith in faith—it is of great therapeutic value. Get up every morning and stand erect in front of an open window, head thrown back, breathe deeply three times, every time with the words, 'I believe, I believe, I believe.' " [6] When faith is reduced to a psychological state, then, salvation comes as a result of one's success in cultivating or maintaining the proper state. Salvation is a reward given to those who attain the correct intensity of faith. People are, therefore, encouraged to believe harder. Those who believe the best and the most are the ones who are saved the best and the most. Faith becomes a "work," and people are thought to be able to justify themselves through the act of faith.

The New Testament, however, insists that the focus of faith is directed toward Someone outside the self: God, the gospel, and the Christ it announces. The faith that is awakened by the gospel is not simply a psychological state which a person can maintain by trying hard or mastering a certain mental attitude, mood, or routine.

The third reductionism insinuates that faith is the opposite of understanding. According to this view, if we have good evidence to prove something, we say we "know" it. If we have only partial evidence, we say we "believe" it. But if we have no evidence at all then we say we have "faith" it is so. This kind of reductionism leaves the impression that faith is the opposite of understanding. Therefore, to be "saved by faith" sounds as if we are being saved by ignorance; one gets the picture of someone who closes his eyes, breathes hard, and believes something in spite of all the evidence to the contrary. Like the writer of Hebrews (Heb. 11:1), John Wesley believed that a form of "evidence" is involved in the nature of Christian faith. However, as quoted in Albert Outler's *John Wesley*, that "evidence" is "not discoverable by our bodily senses" but is rather "a divine evidence or conviction that 'God was in Christ, reconciling the world unto Himself' " (2 Cor. 5:19). Faith is certainly not the opposite of understanding.

Viewing faith as a centered, personal, and relational act of trust and commitment is a biblical antidote to all three of these reductionisms. Wesley saw this clearly. Though he spoke of faith in terms of a "general divine evidence," he always added the personal-relational dimension by saying that faith is "a sure *trust* and confidence that Christ died for *my* sins, that He loved *me* and gave Himself for *me*." [7] Trust is both a verb and a noun. It allows us to say, "She trusts" and "She has trust." Since our very identity is constituted by the pattern or network of trusts that we hold (we *are* what we trust), whatever is accorded our ultimate trust would have to be called our god, whether or not the "truster" is explicitly religious.

To trust God as presented in the gospel and to submit ourselves to the Lordship of Christ is to have all of our previous trusts called into question. If one truly trusts Christ one begins to realign the configuration of trusts that makes one who one is. Therefore, to realign our trusts is to realign life at its very center. The doctrine of justification by faith proclaims that we are rightly related to God by entrusting ourselves to God on the basis of the gospel. That is precisely why trusting the living God redeems life at the center.

Only the person who trusts God, as the gospel presents God,

experiences the gospel as power. Trust is a response of the whole self which comes as a result of hearing the gospel (Rom. 10:17). This hearing, however, is more than confrontation with a body of material. It is confrontation with the living Christ who is known through the gospel. It is this confrontation which calls for response, and the only appropriate response is ultimate trust. To trust someone is to commit one's self. To trust a person is to rely on that person and to allow one's self to be shaped on a deep level by that person. In this sense, it is the object of trust that shapes the "truster." To trust the Christ of the gospel is to rely on him, and to be shaped by him. Whether or not we are Christian depends upon whom or what we trust.

If we would take the Bible seriously and understand faith as trust, we would not need to regard doubt and inquiry so anxiously. For the opposite of faith is not doubt, but distrust or mistrust. Moreover, faith as trust restores the personal dimension. You see, it is possible to believe some*thing*, but trust is reserved for persons. Trust is relational.[8]

It is for this reason that the historic creeds never say, "I believe *that* God exists." So does the devil, and that "belief" doesn't make any difference at all! Many people have what Wesley called a "notional" or "speculative" faith, which is not Christian faith. He says that Christian faith:

> Is not a bare assent to this proposition, Jesus is the Christ; nor indeed to all the propositions contained in our creed, or in the Old and New Testament. It is not merely an assent to any or all these credible things as credible. To say this, were to say (which who could hear?) that the devils were born of God; for they have this faith. They, trembling, believe, both Jesus is the Christ, and that all Scripture, having been given by inspiration of God, is true as God is true.[9]

This, however, is how people respond to the popular religion polls that are taken in America and other parts of the world. Over 90 percent of all Americans say, "Of course we believe that God exists." But, almost half of that 90 percent go on to say that this belief makes no difference in their lives. It is like saying, "Of course I have a neighbor named Ed Walton." But this only asserts my belief in the fact of Walton's existence. That is all. The creeds take a different approach. They say, "I believe *in* God, the Father Almighty. . . ." The little word *in* makes all the difference in the world. If I say, "I believe *in* my neighbor, Ed Walton," this means I am involved in a relational act of trust, commitment, and allegiance. It means that a relational covenant exists between my neighbor and me.

It is obvious that a huge block of those who tell George Gallup that God exists use this "belief" as an inoculation against true faith, vital relational trust in the living God. They have good civil religion, but no Christian faith. It is much easier that way. Almost any religion makes lighter demands than the call to a personal relationship with God. People will accept divinely inspired laws, ideas, or systems of thought, or divinely derived propositions, much sooner than they will accept a personal relationship with the living God. You see, to say "I believe *in* God" means that I trust God; that I commit my allegiance to God; that I covenant with God. It also means that I live out my life under God's righteous judgment, and that impacts my total existence. Therefore, I repent. I turn my life Godward.

In Chapter Two we saw how faith and repentance are the necessary responses to Jesus and his message of the kingdom. Through repentance and faith the saving initiative of God is translated into human experience. We also observed the integral connection between the two. On the one hand, without trusting the divine revelation in Christ there can be no genuine "turning." Trusting the living God is itself a form of turning from other gods and allegiances. On the other hand, radical trust is possible only through a "turning" to God which recognizes personal guilt and the need for grace. Moreover, I tried to show that repentance and faith are more than "prior events"; they are extended acts which include both instantaneous and gradual elements. In addition, "trusting" and "turning" are not just a matter of the soul but involve the total self and the total life. Thus, it is possible to talk about a *life* of repentance and faith—in other words, a process, a turning.

The primary characteristic of this conception of conversion is its dynamic interpretation of life as a pilgrimage over the long pull of years rather than viewing conversion solely in terms of the initial encounter with Christ. In this view there may be many turns all along the way, although there will probably be one initial one-hundred-and-eighty degree turn. This dynamic interpretation is what Orlando Costas has in mind in describing conversion as plunging "into an ongoing adventure":

> Christian conversion is a journey into the mystery of the Kingdom of God which leads from one experience to another. Initiation in the journey of the Kingdom implies a plunge into an eschatological adventure where one is confronted with ever new decisions, turning points, fulfillments, and promises which will continue until the ultimate fulfillment of the Kingdom.[10]

Now it remains necessary to speak more specifically of the nature of repentance as a human response. Just as there are damaging reductionisms to our understanding of faith, there are, likewise, a number of popular ideas that cause us to miss the biblical significance of repentance.

Some see repentance as little more than a once-in-a-lifetime prerequisite for entering the salvation experience. Our oldest daughter, Tonya, used to have a plaque on her bedroom wall which said, "REPENT AND BE SAVED." But at the bottom of the plaque in much smaller type was written, "If you have already repented please disregard this notice." In other words, if one has used repentance as a prerequisite for forgiveness or grace, then, it can be disregarded as part of one's forgotten past. Accordingly, repentance is used as a condition for grace, and the biblical view which sees repentance as a response to grace is totally overlooked. The stark contrast between these views is pointed out by Leander Keck in his comparison of Jesus' understanding of repentance with that of John the Baptist:

> . . . Jesus revolutionizes repentance itself, for whereas John the Baptist required repentance as readiness for the coming of the

Judge, Jesus summoned men to repent as a response to God's Kingdom. Accordingly, in realigning the contours of one's life by trusting Jesus, one appropriates the central thrust of Jesus' own message: repentance as response. Since repentance is neither regret for not being religious sooner, nor remorse requisite for forgiveness, but the steady lifelong process of appropriating Jesus as one's paradigm, repentance holds together faith and ethics, religious trust and moral action. Repentance, so conceived, is not the prelude to Christian existence but the name of the game itself. . . . Because trusting Jesus is not an instantaneous solution but a lifelong process, . . . repentance is a continuum in which trust in Jesus becomes paramount among all other trusts.[11]

The point of Jesus' advent and his message of the kingdom was to prove that forgiveness and grace are freely available in the "now." If this were not true, repentance and faith would not be within the realm of possibility. Were it not for God's revelation in Jesus Christ, conversion would continue as a demand, but it would not be a possibility. And the message of the kingdom would not bring joy beyond all measure but just another demand on top of those we already have. However, since the message of the New Testament is the announcement that the kingdom of God has come in Christ, this signals the fact that the day of repentance-conversion has come.

Repentance then is a response to God's initiative and grace. Therefore, forgiveness and grace do not come as a result of repentance. Repentance comes as a result of God's pardoning grace. Repentance is not done in the hope that God will forgive. It is the fact of God's pardoning grace and the proof of it in the resurrection that causes one to repent. Repentance comes as a response to the good news that God has taken the initiative on our behalf. Being overwhelmed by a sense of gratitude for God's grace, we repent. We turn our lives Godward. We enter upon a life of joyous turning to the Forgiver, a radical new direction in living.

Others mistakenly view repentance as penance. This error comes mostly from the Roman Catholic system of penance. Since penance is said to be necessary in order to receive absolution, penance is viewed as a prerequisite for forgiveness. But, the problem with penance is that it is generally negative. Often it is little more than a matter of regret for not having been religious sooner rather than any positive turning of one's life Godward. Hans Küng, the Roman Catholic scholar, says that repentance is "not a question of 'doing penance' externally, in sackcloth and ashes."[12]

Both of these mistaken notions regarding repentance have tended to make it a "work." They have presented it as a means for pardoning grace rather than the result of it. According to these mistaken views, one must achieve a certain level of repentance before God's pardoning grace is available. Moreover, the assurance of pardon is made dependent on how real and deep-seated one's repentance is. But the life, message, death, and resurrection of Jesus changed all of that. Therefore, one does not have to be a certain kind of person or reach a certain level of repentance in order to be forgiven. God forgives, and that's that! Moreover, God validated and ratified Jesus and his message on forgiveness by raising him from the dead. So it is the resurrection which proves that God's pardoning grace is available and active. Were it not for the resurrection, forgiveness would still be something that people must work for or do penance for.

## CHRISTIAN CONVERSION IS INSTANTANEOUS AND GRADUAL

It is obvious from this description of Christian conversion as a process including prevenient *and* justifying grace, faith *and* repentance, that conversion has both its instantaneous *and* its gradual elements. Mark you, in speaking of conversion as a process no attempt is being made to diminish the reality of initial or threshold experiences. John Wesley, prior to Aldersgate, struggled with the question as to whether or not faith could be given in a moment, or whether or not a person could be instantaneously turned from darkness to light. He said, "I searched the Scriptures again touching this very thing, particularly the Acts of the Apostles: but, to my utter astonishment, found scarce any instances there of other than instantaneous conversions; scarce any so slow as that of St. Paul, who was three days in the pangs of the new birth." [13] Wesley's theology of Christian conversion contained the possibility of a crisis point or threshold.

Just because Christian conversion is a process we do not have to suppose there is not room for crisis points. Crisis points are rooted in the realities of human experience. Just as a journey of a thousand miles begins with the first step, so conversion has a threshold, an initiation, a new beginning. This new beginning is initiated when we confront grace and appropriate faith and turn our lives Godward. If we refuse to trust God and turn from sin toward God, we are not Christian. To appropriate faith means to trust one's life into the hands of a God who has already fought and won the decisive battle against all those powers of evil which attempt to keep everything out of focus. When we stake our lives on this loving God, we cross the threshold and find a new direction.

But even the crossing of the threshold has both its instantaneous and gradual characteristics. Most of us are familiar with those old-fashioned, green, roller-type window shades. Imagine yourself in a room that is darkened because these shades are drawn. How do you get light into the room? You can stumble clumsily in the darkness until you grasp the bottom of the shade, give it a radical yank, and let it go. The shade goes up in a flash, and a penetrating, almost blinding light suddenly floods the room. Or you can make your way through the darkness more carefully and deliberately until you have found the window, grasp the bottom of the shade, give it a gentle tug, hold on to it, and the shade goes up slowly as light gradually fills the room. Now the fundamental thing is not the speed of the shade but the fact that light floods the room!

Joe Hale has helped me understand this phenomenon. He insists that there is found in conversion *both crisis and process* and that both of these aspects are essential to our understanding. Therefore, it is impossible to talk about one without recognizing the other. On the basis of this observation he puts forth the following thesis: "There is no conversion so instantaneous that it completely happens overnight. There is no conversion so gradual that the person is unaware of God's working in him."

In support of the first proposition Hale uses the analogy of marriage. "The courtship may be long or short, but there is a courtship. Even if you walk out of your house, meet a girl on the street and in that instant ask her to marry you, and even if she says 'Yes,' *steps* would have to be taken to lead you to the altar of the church!" Hale concludes: "In our relationship with God, the steps that lead us to commitment may come relatively thick and fast in a brief period or they may be a long line of graduations, a slow process, that prepares the way . . . for conversion."

In support of the second proposition Hale observes: "In a very real sense conversion *is* awareness. Unless we are aware of ourselves, of God, of claims upon our lives as revealed in Christ, it is not meaningful to say that we are Christian. That is why teaching people *about* Christ and the Christian faith is far different from teaching people to *be* Christians. The former can be done without the teacher or the pupil really being personally committed to the subject. The latter requires personal involvement and dedication. . . . It is certainly true that we grow toward understanding and that the capacity for relationship is developed. However, our growing toward relationship leads to awareness, which in this case is the initial step in conversion." Finally, he says, "It may be helpful to think of the gradual turning Godward as the coming of the dawn. We may not know the precise moment, but we know that an hour ago it was dark and now it is light." [14]

As the reader will see in the final chapter, people experience conversion in a variety of ways. The idea that all conversions have to be alike to be valid is erroneous. For some, conversion may come slowly over a long period of time and the person may scarcely remember when he or she made a change. Even so, there is a sense in which a gradual conversion is instantaneous. The sudden enters into the gradual. Those whose experience has been more gradual usually witness to certain occasions which mark distinct progress, as when an illuminating truth has been yielded to or when victories have been won. To this extent the sudden enters the gradual. In others, conversion may clearly be instantaneous. Wesley found that people who had been indifferent to God were suddenly awakened to a sense of their sin and need, and that after going through a period of distressed conviction, they found immediate peace and joy through trusting Christ.[15]

There were strong instantaneous elements in the initial stages of my own Christian pilgrimage. That seems quite true of Paul's experience. No doubt he had an immediate and sudden crisis when he confronted Jesus Christ on the Damascus Road; although it did take several days for the process of new life and vision to take shape. Moreover, God's dealings in Paul's life started before the crisis and continued beyond it, but from his own witness one can judge that on that day Paul crossed a threshold.

Peter seems to have had no instantaneous crisis experience, but rather a series of crises in which he struggled up to the threshold but didn't quite cross it until just before the Ascension and Pentecost. Timothy's experience was probably more gradual than Peter's. He inherited from his grandmother, Lois, and his mother, Eunice, all of the deep convictions of a devout Hebrew family. I'm convinced that his crossing of the threshold was not accompanied by the spectacular, but came quietly in the form of a growing, abiding assurance. Timothy's experience seems more like that of a dear friend of mine. Though he knows the assurance of God's accepting love, he cannot recall ever having any sort of cataclysmic experience. In my travels I have talked with countless people who possess divine assurance but cannot remember the exact day or the hour when they crossed the threshold. All they know is that they're on the other side and life is in focus.[16]

However, "crossing the threshold," either suddenly or gradually, doesn't constitute the end of the journey. If repentance (conversion) is the total turning of one's total life toward the total will of God, then, to be sure, that isn't finished in a flash. Neither can it ever be considered as an absolutely completed journey. "While conversion begins, as everything in history does, at some point in time, the process of conversion is not completed until every aspect of the human personality is driven out into the light of God's mercy, judged, and renewed. . . . Conversion refers not only to the initial moment of faith, no matter how dramatic, . . . but to the whole life of the believer and the network of relationships in which that life is entangled: personal, familial, social, economic, political." [17]

Just because the person takes a "turn" in the right direction doesn't mean that there are not numerous other turns in the ongoing adventure. All along the journey one must be sensitive to the will of God and the promptings of the Holy Spirit, giving more and more of one's total self to God's total will. In other words, total turning necessitates many "turns" in one's pilgrimage. This process of turning, however, signals a new direction, a new life-style in which one's commitment to God, through Jesus Christ, changes one's whole life. It means both internal and external change. The whole person in all his or her relationships is transformed by God's grace. And whether gradual or instantaneous, Christian conversion is always the work of God. There is the human response, but it is response to what has already been initiated by God.

But Christian conversion means more than turning one's whole self toward God's will. As we observed earlier, it also means turning away from those things that tyrannize us and cause our lives to be "out of focus." It involves a *terminus-a-quo* and a *terminus-ad-quem*, that is, a turning from something and a turning toward something. To be in focus means that we are neither enamored by nor mesmerized by personal idolatries or public powers. We have turned our backs on such personal sins as promiscuity, hate, prejudice, drugs, selfishness, greed, and lust. Moreover, we will no longer endorse such public sins as political and military tyranny, corruption, economic exploitation, racial injustice, and dehumanizing technocracy. The life which has been brought into focus by the grace of God in Christ must resist these evils. But, how do we acquire the power to turn from evil?

## CHRISTIAN CONVERSION MEANS PARDON AND POWER

The abundant grace of God provides more than pardon; it provides power. Therefore, Christian conversion has to do with power over sin as well as pardon of sin. Grace is both "favor toward" and "power in." To highlight one of these to the exclusion of the other is to bifurcate the "wholeness" of the gospel and Christian experience. Exclusive emphasis on grace as pardon generally leads the church to "cheap grace" and antinomianism. "In such a Church the world finds a cheap covering for its sins; no contribution is required, still less any real desire to be delivered from sin. Cheap grace, therefore, amounts to a denial of the living Word of God. . . . (It) means the justification of sin without the justification of the repentant sinner who departs from sin and from whom sin departs." [18] Exclusive emphasis on grace as power often falls prey to the error of "salvation by works," and the human pride that accompanies all forms of self-salvation.[19]

John Wesley struck a creative balance between grace as power and grace as pardon. Theodore Runyon's treatment of this balance is most helpful. He points out the attempt by Wesley to show how "the role of justification is to provide the foundation *in* grace for the actual transformation of the person," and how "a qualitative change in human existence is the divine objective in the process of reconciliation." [20] When we receive the gift of faith, we are "justified," or pardoned of all sin. But God is not deceived into thinking that those whom he justifies are actually righteous, fully transformed in their lives and without sin. However, God forgives and "treats" us as if we had not sinned.[21] In response to God's grace we "trust" and "turn."

Now this understanding of justification by faith is not to be taken as a device for evading righteousness, but a new way of realizing it. It is the means of participating in a righteousness which already exists, the perfect righteousness of Christ. In Wesley's terms, to be justified is the act of God *for* us, but this action of God leads to an act of God *in* us—a change of heart, an inward renewal. This change is what Wesley called new birth or regeneration, an inward change from wickedness to goodness. Therefore, grace is more than pardon; it is power. For Wesley, justification and the new birth are related but they are different, concurrent in time but distinctive:

But though it be allowed, that justification and the new birth are, in point of time, inseparable from each other, yet are they easily distinguished, as being not the same, but things of a widely different nature. Justification implies only a relative, the new birth a real change. God in justifying us does something *for* us; in begetting us again, he does the work *in* us. The former changes our outward relation to God, so that of enemies we become children; by the latter our inmost souls are changed, so that of sinners we become saints. The one restores us to the favor, the other to the image of God. The one is the taking away the guilt, the other the taking away the power, of sin: so that, although they are joined together in point of time, yet are they wholly distinct natures.[22]

At the same time a person is justified and born again, sanctification begins. Wesley taught that justification was also the first part or the "gate" of sanctification.[23] He says:

In that instant we are "born again, born from above, born of the spirit." This is a real as well as a relative change. We are inwardly renewed by the power of God. We feel the love of God shed abroad in our heart by the Holy Ghost which is given unto us (Rom. 5:5), producing love to all mankind, and more especially to the children of God, expelling the love of the world, the love of pleasure, of ease, of honour, of money, together with pride, anger, self-will and every other evil temper.[24]

It is important to note that sanctification only "begins" with justification and the new birth; it is not complete; sin still remains. The Christian is justified, but sin, though it does not reign, nevertheless, remains in the heart. Therefore, continuous repentance is necessary for Christian growth. Even the Christian who has reached "perfection" is a sinner as judged by the *perfect* will of God, and needs continual repentance. Wesley says,

There is also a repentance and faith . . . which are requisite after we have "believed the Gospel"; yea, and in every subsequent stage of our Christian course, or we cannot "run the race which is set before us." And this repentance and faith are as full and necessary, in order to our continuance and growth in grace, as former faith and repentance were, in order to our entering the Kingdom of God.[25]

There must be a continual "turning" or reorientation of life, and this is not contradictory to the work of sanctification, since sanctification is a process of growth in God's grace in which our actions are more and more governed by the work of grace in us. Thus, sanctification is analogous to a baby which is born in a moment, but grows into maturity only gradually.[26]

According to Wesleyan theology, therefore, God both imputes and imparts righteousness. God pardons and remits the punishment due our sins, restoring us to favor and restoring our dead souls to spiritual life.[27] "Christians are not just declared righteous, they are regenerated, endowed by the Spirit and nurtured through the means of grace actually to become what they are declared to be." [28] Wesley believed that the conversion process resulted in the actual transformation of the human condition. Justification leads to sanctification; righteousness imputed to righteousness imparted; pardon of sin to power over sin.

Paul's conversion illustrates this truth. Here we get a historic illustration of the power of God to intervene in the life of a man who was persecuting the church, attacking the gospel, denying the resurrection. If God can rectify a person like Paul, God can do anything.

Paul was religious before his Christian conversion. His was a religion of moral rectitude which got its theological support from his pharisaism. God ignored Paul's bad theology, however, and broke through to Paul on God's own terms. This means that God has the power to break through to us no matter how twisted our theology or our lives. God did not wait until Paul had straightened out his theology or his life. Such a god would be thwarted by false theology and shallow life and powerless to act. Such a god would be reduced to a passive deity wishing things would be better for us but unable to act until we first toe the line. But Paul's conversion attests to the fact that God is powerful enough to do something even about a person like Paul. From this we learn that the Redeemer acts on behalf of people like Paul because God is committed to making creation right. As a result, Paul can say that it is God's kindness which leads to repentance (Rom. 2:4).

The conversion of Paul resulted in a changed Paul. The proud persecutor of the Christians turned to Christ and joined the Christian community. He discovered a new center for his life. As a result, he changed his way of thinking and living. His mind was remade and his whole nature transformed (Rom. 12:2). His concept of salvation was radically altered because of his encounter with Christ. Paul experienced grace both as pardon and as power.

Moreover, as Runyon points out, the inherent goal and purpose of all of this pardoning and empowerment is not directed primarily toward heaven, but the "refashioning of life in this world."

> Typically, Protestants see justification or conversion as the decisive, revolutionary event. Wesley would agree. But then, just as typically, the revolution becomes the maypole around which the rest of life is danced, rather than a bench mark that sets the course of the future that is to be built.[29]

There is a larger goal in God's working to transform us. God knows that only changed people can build and maintain a changed world. No economic device or political contraption will work better without better people. Individuals who are problems to themselves will not solve the world's problems. God holds us accountable for building a better world.

Since conversion is only the "bench mark" that sets our course, accountability does not end at justification. It only begins there. For salvation to be real, it must work its way out in terms of the relationships of this world. This is why Wesley envisioned a *Christian world*, a society of economic justice, where "they cannot suffer one among them to lack anything, but continually give to every man as he hath need." [30] Anything less is not "Scriptural Christianity."

Religion is not to be viewed, therefore, as alienated humanity's means of escape to a more tolerable, heavenly realm, but as participation in God's own redemptive enterprise, transforming alienated servants into liberated sons and daughters, whose works are at one and the same time the expression of their own life in the Spirit and the sign of the new age of justice and love that is to come.[31]

Wesley would have disagreed with the understanding of conversion espoused by some who teach that conversion results only in getting the soul ready for heaven but does not effect any essential change in the individual's social nature. This narrow emphasis causes people to claim to be "saved" while they remain self-centered, acquisitive, and totally bound to all the cultural values that thwart God's vision of *shalom*. As a matter of fact, their exclusive emphasis on individualistic "soul" salvation makes them suspicious of any interest in community or social transformation. In this respect they would appear to agree with the cynics, pessimists and determinists that human nature is an unchangeable given and salvation comes only to a portion of human life, the soul, and not the whole person. But, Christian conversion means both pardon and power. God sent Jesus Christ into the world not just to get us ready to die but ready to live; not just to get us into heaven but to get heaven into us; not just to keep us out of hell but to keep hell out of us. Since God's power transforms us into new persons, those who pledge allegiance to God are not just among the especially privileged but among the especially responsible.

## CHRISTIAN CONVERSION MEANS
## FULFILLING A NEW RESPONSIBILITY

Christian conversion must include turning to other people as well as to God, the love of neighbor as well as the love of God. Leslie Newbigin contends,

Neither the teaching of the Old Testament prophets, nor that of the Gospel . . . provides any basis for the view of conversion which is very common among Christians, namely, that conversion is some sort of purely inward and spiritual experience which is later followed by a distinct and different decision to act in certain ways. The idea that one is first converted, and then looks around to see what one should do as a consequence, finds no basis in Scripture. . . . Conversion means being turned around in order to recognize and participate in the dawning reality of God's reign. But this inward turning immediately and intrinsically involves both a pattern of conduct and a physical companionship. It involves membership in a community and a decision to act in certain ways. . . . Thus the three elements to which we have referred are present from the beginning as intrinsic elements in the total fact of conversion: an inward turning of the heart and mind, commitment to a visible fellowship, and commitment to a kind of conduct.[32]

Gabriel Fackre offers an antidote for the peril of trying to separate love for God from love for neighbor. He says that involvement in redemptive ministries is not just that which happens *eventually* after a person's conversion. Rather, "the authenticity of conversion is marked by the presence in it of the ultimate goal of it. 'The end preexists in the means.' As Emerson observes in another context . . . what eventuates is controlled by what initiates. . . . The outcome sought is visible in the route toward it." Fackre goes on to say, if the ground and goal of conversion, "the target of turning, is the God of Shalom who wills not only a new person, but a new community and a new earth, then, the act of orienting to that vision must manifest in itself those characteristics." [33]

This means that involved in and subsequent to the "threshold" aspect of Christian conversion is the matter of one's relationship to one's neighbor. Put another way, it means that implicit in the "threshold" experience is not only a vertical relationship with God but also a horizontal relationship with one's neighbor. Again, consistent with our holistic concept of conversion, a change of one's heart cannot be real apart from a change of one's relationships. Christian conversion includes both individual persons and the relationships in which those persons live. It "includes soul and body, the individual as well as his community, his own way of life as well as the system in which he lives. Conversion is in tendency as universal as the Kingdom of God, in whose imminence it is both made possible and demanded." [34] Conversion to God and the neighbor occur as one and the same process, and both aspects are dependent upon God's revelation in Christ. "Without Christ we should not know God, we could not call upon Him, nor come to Him. But without Christ we also would not know our brother, nor could we come to him. The way is blocked by our own ego. Christ opened up the way to God and to our brother." [35]

Therefore, working to liberate the oppressed and serving the wretched of the earth are part and parcel of Christian conversion. Since conversion always takes place within the context of concrete history, the validity of one's conversion is attested by the power to deal with society's most concrete and entrenched social sins. Where this element is absent, we have grounds to suspect whether we have actually had our lives brought into focus by God. Genuine Christian conversion causes the heart to throb with a compassion to put one's life at God's disposal (Rom. 6:12-19). Since God is at work in the world freeing the oppressed, feeding the hungry, clothing the naked, visiting the sick and imprisoned, and ministering to the aged, how can we do less than position ourselves alongside this suffering, serving, loving God? It was this divine compassion and compulsion that E. Stanley Jones witnessed at his conversion. He said, "The universe opened its arms and took me in. I felt as though I wanted to put my arms around the whole world." [36]

Thus the Christian gospel declares God's liberating news for all creation. God's salvation is "big"! It is as universal as the kingdom of God. God is not only determined to save individuals, God is determined to save the whole universe and bring about "a new heaven and a new earth" (Rev. 21:1). God is the God of *shalom*, and the person whose life has been focused by God shares that vision and prays and works for its realization.

Now it is obvious that anything as radical as Christian conversion cannot happen in a vacuum. The authentic Christian life is so strenuous that it cannot be lived out in the world without the power of God and the support of a community of those whose lives are being focused by God.

## CHRISTIAN CONVERSION MEANS ENTERING A NEW FELLOWSHIP

John Baillie once said, "I cannot be a Christian all by myself. I cannot retire into my own shell or into my own corner and live the Christian life. A single individual cannot be a Christian in his singleness." [37] I agree. However, I seldom ever visit a place that I do not hear someone say, "You don't have to be a part of a local church in order to be Christian." This is a popular "cop-out." It is a part of the contemporary passion for anonymity, the desire to be right with God and, at the same time, avoid human community. There are millions who wish to believe without belonging.[38] Obviously, it is much easier that way. It is easier to sit at home on Sunday morning, sip a cup of coffee, "watch" a worship service in one's pajamas, and get on a television evangelist's mailing list, than it is to involve oneself in the "nitty-gritty" testing ground of a local church.

Certainly a part of the responsibility for the fact that some people leave mainline churches can be laid at the doors of the churches themselves. According to Dudley's illuminating study, when the individual believer comes to our churches he or she "expects fulfillment through personal faith, individual responsibility, and continued growth 'in the nurture and admonition of God.'" When these needs are disappointed, people's hunger for Christian experience and maturity leads them elsewhere. Dudley contends that, "No studies have been able to demonstrate that church membership was responsible for changing individuals from those in need to those who were happier." [39]

However, persons who think the local church is unnecessary are not cognizant of the fact that a part of the New Testament understanding of Christian conversion involves incorporation into a local community of faith. To misconstrue conversion as an isolated, individualistic experience without any reference to the local church, is to do irrevocable damage to the biblical concept of Christian conversion. John Wesley once said, "To turn Christianity into a solitary religion is to destroy it." [40] God wills not only a new person but a new community, a community of celebration, mutual support, serving, and witnessing. Christ's invitation to conversion is immediately followed by his call to discipleship. His proclamation of the coming kingdom was matched by his creation of a new community which would be the "first fruit" of that kingdom, the visible manifestation of the beginning of the realization of God's dream of *shalom*. As Paul Löffler has said, "Conversion to Christ without the Church decapitates the head from the Body. Conversion must lead into the Church." [41]

During an evangelistic mission a middle-aged woman, who had withdrawn her membership from her church ten years previously, committed her life to Christ and expressed the desire to be reinstated as a member in The United Methodist Church. She confessed that she had withdrawn earlier because she couldn't agree with the denomination's Social Creed. She admitted her mistake with these words: "I've got to join in order to survive! I've learned that you can't be Christian or human alone."

And you can't! For this reason, the church is more than just an organization charged with the responsibility to communicate the gospel by word and deed. The church is actually part and parcel of the *evangel*, the good news of God. The church is a part of what God has done in order to meet the deep needs of human beings. To speak, therefore, of conversion without incorporation into the life of the church also decapitates the gospel. For to really be in Christ is to be in Christ's church. I agree with William Barclay:

> There ought to be a much closer connexion between conversion and the Church. It is the strange and odd fact that as things now are it is not in the Church that we expect to find conversions happening. We have actually come to a state of things when we expect to find conversions happening at missions and campaigns outside the Church rather than within the ordinary work, ministry, and activity of the Church. . . . Conversion will

never be what it was meant to be until it happens within the Church, and the Church will never be what it was meant to be until each [person] who enters it, enters it in conscious and deliberate decision.[42]

According to the New Testament, awareness of one's individual identity before God necessarily involves one in community. Life in the Spirit of Christ is the life of new openness to others in a fellowship of reconciliation. This new identity is found "in Christ." The risen Christ gives us a new perception of the inter-relation of individuals and community. Individuals are related to the community by virtue of a relationship to Christ. As Norman Kraus puts it, "They achieve their self-identity in the community through identification with Him." [43] This new identity is not to be found outside the community. "There is no more possibility of personal identity apart from the brother than there is of loving Christ without loving the brother" (1 John 4:20).[44] This teaches us that the individual's new personal identity as a Christian or new self-awareness as being "saved" is formed through identification with Christ in his Body, the church. Therefore, a part of the evangelistic call is to turn from independency, self-sufficiency, and pride that characterizes human beings in their individualism and to submit to the Lordship of Jesus Christ within his new messianic community, the church.

So, the biblical pattern is not a detached individual savoring his or her own private religious experience. It is rather new crea-tions in Christ who necessarily involve themselves in responsible participation in our Lord's church. If we take the Bible seriously, we dare not make the mistake of discounting the corporate reality and influence of the local church. The church is the Body of Christ. So the church of Jesus Christ in its local expression is essential. Certainly, this understanding of the essential nature of the local church need not blind us to its awesome weaknesses or bind us to local church structures to the extent that we are not free to work and minister in the world. Just as the mother bird does not hatch her eggs by the weight of her body, but by its warmth, and as the egg does not complete the cycle of its species within the nest, but in the world, so the church must conceive its corporate identity within the context of the kingdom of God and its evangelizing power as an unbridled Spirit unconfined by walls and rituals.

From the beginning our attempt has been to show how Christian conversion has both its individual and communal sides. Christian baptism is a powerful symbol of this. Baptism and conversion are always linked in the New Testament. Wherever one is mentioned the other is somewhere near to be found. We will not attempt here an extensive examination of the doctrine of Christian baptism.[45] That would require another book. Suffice it to say that the close link between the New Testament understanding of conversion and the necessity for baptism serves to highlight the place of the church in the scheme of redemption. It is the church that administers baptism.

Michael Green calls our attention to the various ways Christian baptism is presented in the New Testament:

> It was the mark of incorporation within the Body of Christ— "by one Spirit we were all baptized into one Body." It was the mark of purification, of cleansing from the old sins. It was the mark of justification—"you were washed, you were sanctified, you were justified in the name of the Lord Jesus." . . . It was the mark of the new covenant. . . . It was initiation into the realm of the Spirit. . . . It meant such a close union with Christ that the believer was a participant in His death and resurrection.[46]

Baptism was given by the New Testament church when a person professed faith and repentance. It was a sign of God's forgiveness and the empowerment by the Spirit. Moreover, it initiated a person into a new community which shared a common life and ministry.

This continues to be the process by which "outsiders" are brought to faith and incorporation. At a time in which the majority population is "unchurched," this process must continue as a primary thrust in the church's evangelism. Otherwise, major populations will never be reached. The church's standard "biological growth" or "nurturing" concepts are not adequate for the conversion of huge numbers of persons who are outside the community of faith. The process outlined in the New Testament is far more appropriate for this task.

This in no way denies the validity of infant baptism for those who are born to Christian parents and brought up in the ranks of the church. For such, infant baptism is a symbol of justification by faith. It symbolizes the fact that faith is a response to God's saving activity. It is a powerful recognition that God has accepted us even when we are weak, helpless infants. Our affirmation of the baptism of infants underscores the most important thing in all baptism, whether infant, youth, or adult, and that is God's divine action. For those fortunate enough to have been born into Christian homes, baptized, and nurtured in the Christian church, the conversion process unfolds as maturing children move through different stages of faith and eventually come to "own" the faith for themselves.[47] But with any age baptism signifies the absolutely indispensable place of the Christian community and highlights the fact that Christian conversion means entering a new fellowship.

In Chapters Seven and Eight I have tried to show that Christian conversion is a multi-faceted dynamic process which defies simplistic interpretation. How we approach conversion depends greatly upon our angle of vision, and our angle of vision is greatly influenced by our particular context. In the next chapter I will spell out how this biblical understanding of Christian conversion as dynamic process is sometimes subject to being undermined and inhibited.

## QUESTIONS FOR THOUGHT AND DISCUSSION

1. The author defines Christian faith as "a centered, personal, and relational act of trust and commitment" (p. 116). How would you amplify this statement? Revise it?

2. Pages 116-119 outline three ways in which the meaning of

"faith" is reduced. Describe each. What can you do to counter these distortions?

3. Based on the understanding of repentance here, you might make two lists: "Repentance Is Not . . .," and "Repentance Is . . . ."

4. Conversion is interpreted as both instantaneous and gradual, as involving crisis points as well as a continuing process. Can you illustrate this with your own experience or that of someone you know?

5. Likewise, conversion is seen as both pardon and power, as grace that both delivers us from sin and transforms us, setting us on a new course toward righteousness, sanctification, and *shalom*. Give a personal example.

6. After conversion who is our neighbor? And what is our responsibility to this neighbor?

7. How would you answer someone who says, "Once people are converted they don't really need the church anymore"?

# 9. Inhibitors of Christian Conversion

In framing an understanding of Christian conversion we have attempted to (1) concentrate upon the normative position of the gospel of Jesus Christ; (2) give serious consideration to the importance of context; (3) highlight the fact that our triune God is the Author of every aspect of conversion; (4) show how the living God has communicated redemptive love in the gospel of Jesus Christ; (5) portray the seriousness of sin as contagious disease and cumulative effect; and (6) affirm that Christian conversion is a multi-faceted, dynamic process through which the living God enables creation to realize the promise of *shalom*.

Throughout the book we have attempted to steer clear of the following: (1) too much emphasis on conversion as a single act; (2) the imbalance which comes from making human experience the final arbiter of the gospel; (3) the temptation to reduce theology to ideology; (4) the attempt to confine the dynamics of God's dealings with people to precut orders, forms, or plans; and (5) the attempt to stereotype a specific kind of experience and impose that upon everyone without regard to the biblical perspective, the uniqueness of personality, or the particularity of context. Any number of things are capable of causing us to miss this dynamic interpretation of Christian conversion.

## MORPHOLOGICAL IDOLATRY

"Morphology" is the study of biological forms and structures. Sometimes the church tends to overemphasize forms and structures to the point of idolatry. One primary inhibitor to Christian conversion is the inability to differentiate between cultural and traditional forms of conversion developed throughout the church's history, and the biblical concept of conversion. This inability is coupled with too much emphasis put upon conversion as a single act. Both distortions lead to an understanding of conversion which has lost its comprehensive meaning for the ongoing and total renewal of life and culture.

Much of the impetus for this misunderstanding is traceable to that movement in church history called Protestant scholasticism. Yielding to the influence of rationalism, the church sought an understanding of conversion that could be stated in precise, clear-cut cognitive categories. As a result, conversion began to lose some of its fluid, dynamic sense and was confined to one logical, narrow activity in the so-called "order of salvation." Categories such as justification and sanctification and conversion became fixed, somewhat disconnected acts of initiation into salvation. Great debates ensued over which came first. Everything had to coincide with carefully worked out rational and logical orders.

The pietist and Puritan movements strongly reinforced this emphasis by placing heavy stress upon individualistic experiential salvation. When all of these influences converged, the church was left with a narrow, static, restrictive concept of conversion that did not do justice to the biblical understanding. Eventually, this inherited theological framework became a "straitjacket" that conceived of conversion as "a rigid sequence of moments which, rather than helping to deploy the richness of the one, yet manifold grace of God, forced Christian experience into a pre-established pattern." [1] The artificiality of this morphological idolatry tended to obscure and distort both the unity of the gospel and the unity of the human being.

Eventually this precut pattern became even more wooden, mechanical, and legalistic as it was translated into the revivalism of the late nineteenth and early twentieth centuries. For many revivalist preachers the "order of salvation" was backstaged by an even more restrictive "plan of salvation." This phrase was often used to denote a step-by-step rigid system of conversion. Rigidity developed despite the fact that many of the earlier preachers were sensitive to this issue and warned against any attempt to "strait-jacket" the action of God in a person's life:

Jonathan Edwards insisted that there was no definite order in the process by which a person comes to God. He said, "There is an endless variety in the particular manner and circumstances in which persons are wrought on, and an opportunity of seeing so much of such a work of God will show that God is further from confining Himself to certain steps and a particular method in His work on souls, than it may be some imagine. . . . The work of God has been glorious in its variety." [2] Again Edwards said, "God has appeared far from limiting Himself to any certain method in His proceedings with sinners." [3] Moreover, neither Finney, nor Moody, nor Spurgeon advised a *rigid* plan in instruction to Christians who were being equipped to witness to others. Moody's flexible spirit is indicated by his conviction that God never repeats Himself; He does not approach any two people the same way.[4]

But as the twentieth century progressed, these flexible approaches diminished. While some moved away from any crisis experience, others developed stylized plans of salvation. As long as people registered assent to the plan, they were converted. In practice, the plan sounded something like this: "Do you believe that this book (the Bible) is God's Word?" If the answer was yes, the evangelist then pointed to passages which outlined the "plan of salvation": All are lost (Rom. 3:23); Christ died for our sins (John 3:16); confession of faith brings salvation (Acts 2:36; 16:31). After the plan was presented, the hearers were asked to make a verbal confession of faith and pray a prayer, often printed on a brochure. Once they gave their consent to the plan of salvation, the evangelist then assured them of salvation. Sometimes this boiled down to little more than passive assent to the evangelist's scriptural quotations and words printed on a brochure or tract.

Certain words were given an almost magical power. This is often the case. Words in use over a long period of time gain a reality for themselves which is not always justified. People bow to the illusion that they can capture the power of the living God or

Christ in certain words. I saw this illustrated at a lay conference. During one session, a colleague was leading a discussion on "Christian experience." He was attempting to couch his remarks in an idiom that the uninitiated could understand. One lady became restless with this and began to doubt the authenticity of the leader's conversion. The leader wasn't using any of the magic words. Finally, the lady said, "Well, I just want to know one thing: Are you washed in the blood of the Lamb?" The leader was momentarily nonplussed, but replied, "I am a disciple of Jesus Christ. I know he has forgiven me. I love him with all my heart and have pledged to follow Him always." This seemed to me to be a legitimate response, but the lady was not satisfied. She said, "You didn't answer the question. Are you or are you not washed in the blood of the Lamb?" The leader, in the kindest manner, proceeded to repeat his answer. With that, the dear sister stormed out of the room and refused to attend any more sessions "led by that man." "He is not a Christian," she said. Moreover, she tried to get others to boycott his sessions. This lady had fallen prey to a subtle gnostic heresy, "salvation by words." My colleague refused to play her game. If he had repeated her formula he would have been in her good graces because he would have used the secret gnosis that opens the hidden mysteries of the universe. When he refused he found himself on her "hit-list"!

There are a number of obvious limitations to morphological idolatry. One limitation is the tendency to concentrate on a plan or method and neglect the person. This works both ways. First, conversion is not just acceptance of a plan but confrontation with a person and a kingdom. Second, Jesus did not respond to every person in the same way, as if people were a company of clones. Jesus related to particular persons. In the final analysis the New Testament is the best resource for illustrating the infinite variety of ways in which people are converted. There seems to be no uniformity in New Testament conversions. No form or structure is divinized. Different people register saving faith in different ways. Moreover, there is no typical physical manifestation accompanying New Testament conversions, nor is there only one way by which persons are brought to faith.

Jesus' approach to different individuals is evidence of this. He always makes it a point to take into consideration the background of the individual. The person's training, prejudices, moral status—all of these things were considered, and Jesus' approach was suited to the specific needs of persons with different backgrounds. It is fascinating to note that there is little similarity in Jesus' approach to the woman at the well, Nicodemus, and Nathaniel. Jesus had no stereotyped methods, no elaborate creedal requirements. He adapted his methods to suit community and individual needs. Anyone who imagines that a certain formula or method must be adhered to before a Christian conversion can take place ought to study afresh the life of Jesus.

Years of experience as an evangelist have taught me that people tend to define *conversion* methodologically. That is to say, they assume that conversion is that method by which they themselves or the majority of people in their primary group have come to faith. The method does not have to be understood in a dramatic or cataclysmic fashion. John R. Hendrick, in his excellent book, tells how congregations and denominations develop a limited number of standardized approaches. For many churches it is the communicant or confirmation route, and busloads of children are driven down that route every Lenten season. For others it is the revivalist route, and conversion can only take place once or twice a year when the evangelist comes to town. For others conversion can only happen in small groups where a counseling approach to personal witnessing is used. Hendrick rightly acknowledges that all of these are ways God uses to bring people to faith. But, he insists that no *one* way is *the* way, and goes on to say "that if our approaches are too few or too standardized, we can often be guilty of making the spirits of children and adults fit our precut patterns. God's ways are too unlimited for such methodological narrowness." [5]

One of the church's most deadly diseases is the stereotype. It is like a mental graven image which keeps us from seeing what *is* by encouraging us to concentrate on what we want to see. This presumes to make the mysterious work of God align itself with our mental constructs and thwarts conversion as new possibility.

When this disease becomes chronic, conversion is demanded as mere conformity, a conformity which appeals only to those who are content with fossilized minds and spirits. The convert must conform uncritically to a particular stereotype or method. usually "adorned with the trappings of piety." [6] Few things are more capable of undercutting the biblical understanding of conversion and reducing the gospel to an enslaving system.

Another limitation of morphological idolatry comes at the point of losing the unity or wholeness of the conversion process. Salvation is one work, not a random collection of bits and pieces. It is one thing to attempt to understand the process by delineating stages in development, facets of experience, or what Barth calls different moments and different aspects of the work of God. But, it is something else to break the unitary nature of the conversion process by treating it in a piecemeal fashion. Again, Barth says, "The action of God in his reconciliation of the world unto himself in Jesus Christ is unitary. . . . Whether we look at it from the one standpoint or the other our knowledge can and may and must be a knowledge of the one totality of the reconciling action of God, of the one whole and undivided Jesus Christ, and of His one grace." [7]

A third limitation is the temptation to fix on one or the other points in the "plan of salvation" or "order of salvation" to the exclusion of others. This usually results in lifting out one point and absolutizing it. Gabriel Fackre summarizes the results of this distortion:

The wrenching moment of turning—repentance—produces penitents who dwell remorselessly on the pains and joys of tearing loose. These are the pietists. Others have fixed on belief as the be-all and end-all of the Christian life, interpreting conversion as the rigid acceptance of doctrine. These are the dogmatists. There are also those turners who discover the community aspect of conversion (a life together that may run from the intense group experience to the routines of ecclesiastical existence), and absolutize it. These might be called the groupists. Finally, there are those who find their conversion identity in the doing and serving dimension, and have eyes for nothing else. These are the activists. Pietists, dogmatists, groupism, activism—each treats the part as a whole and in so doing shreds the whole cloth of conversion.[8]

A final limitation produced by morphological idolatry can be seen in the way it strips down the gospel so that all that is left is a call to easy "believism." Some say, "All you have to do is follow the plan and say yes to Jesus. It's one, two, three, four—just like that, and right down the Roman road you go." This approach may lead to "decision" but not necessarily to discipleship. "Church growth" theorists are right in saying, "We deceive ourselves if we believe that a person who has made a decision for Christ, who has prayed 'I accept Jesus Christ into my life,' has truly become a disciple. . . . A *decision* suggests a brief moment of time; a *disciple* suggests a lifelong task. . . . Unless those who make 'decisions for Christ' become active disciples, responsible members of the Church, their decision usually fades rapidly into oblivion." [9]

In addition, easy believism fails to tell the people that faith cannot be understood apart from faithfulness; that conversion leads to costly obedience, radical discipleship. It means a total reorientation of one's life. It means trust and fidelity focused upon Christ and the kingdom of God. To omit any mention of this costly discipleship is dishonest. If Jesus felt it was necessary to point out the cost of discipleship (Luke 14:25-35), can we do less? It is not by one cross we are saved but two, "Christ's and our own." [10] Christian conversion insists that new life is born from a grave, and there is no way to bypass Gethsemane and Calvary. Therefore, Christian conversion is not a selfish turning inward, it is a turning toward Christ and his kingdom, toward the Christian community, toward a lost world and toward God's own dream for creation.

The sheer comprehensiveness and mystery of the biblical understanding of conversion makes it difficult to schematize it and describe it in logical terms. We can be thankful, however, that no matter what may be the origin and goal of conversion or which factor may be first and which second, or where the preponderance may lie, conversion does at any rate take place.[11]

## INDIVIDUALISM

Another inhibitor to Christian conversion is individualism. The Wesleyan movement's emphasis upon the individual has had both its positive and negative sides. One of the movement's greatest strengths has been its emphasis upon a dynamic, satisfying, personal relationship with God which gives peace, motivation, guidance, and strength to the individual. It has stressed an immediate relationship with God, personal assurance of God's presence and power, a strong reliance upon God's guidance, plus individual submission to God's will. Thus, "the people called Methodists" have waged a campaign to bring individuals to commitment to Christ and have inspired converts to win others in personal evangelism. We have insisted upon deep personal piety and moral conscience. These emphases have helped to make us activistic, gregarious, and democratic, and I am grateful to stand in this vital tradition.

But, while our church has reaped great benefits from these characteristics, at times even the strengths of these characteristics have contained the seeds of seductive temptation. We have often been tempted to reduce this emphasis on a personal relationship to God to a form of individualism which has blighted the Wesleyan movement and to some degree severed us from our historical roots. As a result, making conversion a private concern has become endemic.

In its simplest form individualism means "a system or condition in which each individual works for his own ends, in either social, political or religious matters." [12] By definition this implies that self-centeredness is the chief value of life. For some it becomes the goal and shape of religion. This has devastating implications when it is baptized and taken into the church. It is especially damaging when it impacts our understanding of conversion.

First, conversion then becomes the process by which we bring Jesus into our world in order to possess him and use him for individualistic purposes. Conversion is understood as an experience aimed solely at meeting the needs, wants, and desires of the convert. Thus the attempt is made to use Jesus to solve emotional and health problems, get rid of excess fat, deal with hang-ups, hangovers, and worries. The hallmark of conversion becomes success. It offers a quick and easy shortcut to our heart's desires. "Being saved" is understood as being problem-free. All doubts are resolved, hostilities ended. Life is now enchanting and full of wonder. Jesus has solved every problem and promises to supply everything we always wanted. So, conversion results in peace of mind, prosperity, social acceptance, publicity, and success. All this on earth and heaven besides!

The greatest inadequacy in this approach is its essential selfishness, the fact that it is mainly concerned to save the individual.[13] It is a form of infantile narcissism which causes us constantly to confuse our selfish wants with our basic needs, such that we adopt the individualistic, consumer-oriented message and lifestyle of the world and bring it over into the church. Instead of earnestly loving God, we are in love with ourselves and our own salvation.

Second, when individualism runs rampant, conversion happens only in the individual self, a strictly personal experience. I agree with Steven Neill when he says, "At no point can the individual factor in conversion be eliminated." [14] But when the individual factor becomes "individualism" it plays havoc with the church. Conversion becomes pure subjectivity, an experience which happens to individuals in their inner being, in their aloneness, in their isolation from the world and other persons. As an affair of pure subjectivity it results in a change of personal diposition but has little if any significant impact upon the affairs of the world. This distortion results in a privatization of the gospel, an excessively individualistic interpretation that sanctions or ignores the injustices and dehumanizing trends that are built into the structures and institutions of our total life. This represses a major portion of the gospel. It makes people blind to the evil in the structures of society. It attempts to call people out of sinful social structures while leaving the structures untouched. This is like telling a typhoid patient to drink pure water while leaving the only well in town polluted.

The world Methodist family had a dramatic illustration of this attempt to dichotomize the Christian faith when Alan Walker,

Director of the World Evangelism Committee of The World Methodist Council, was ordered out of South Africa some time ago. He was instructed to "start packing his bags and go home" because he condemned an apartheid system of racial segregation. Though he made his case on the basis of the Bible and Christian doctrine, his sermons were called "mere political speeches" by those who were the guardians of injustice. Walker responded, "There is no greater menace in the Church than a born-again Christian without a social conscience." [15] He is right, and a major reason for this dichotomous development is the reduction of conversion to individualism. The gospel becomes ethic-less, bereft of the rigorous virtues of truth and justice and reduced to a sentimental, individualistic, private affair between God and the isolated, insulated self.

The impact of individualism is illustrated by one woman who tells of the results of her conversion: "I was a new creature in Christ Jesus. Everything seemed heavenly rather than earthly: everything was so lovely. . . . It was such a blessed experience, going home I walked on the curbstone rather than walk or talk with ungodly people." [16]

Perhaps there is a larger significance than we have hitherto thought to the fact that Jesus met with Moses and Elijah atop the mountain of transfiguration.[17] Luke says they spoke with Jesus concerning his "exodus" (literally) which was to be accomplished in Jerusalem. To the Jews, the word *exodus* could mean only one thing: "a deliverance." So Moses and Elijah spoke with Jesus concerning the deliverance he was to put in motion in Jerusalem. Here were two men who were representative of more than the law and the prophets. Moses, himself, was the leader of an exodus, a deliverance of God's people from the physical bondage and oppression of Egypt. Likewise, Elijah was the leader of an exodus. When the people of God were in spiritual bondage, worshiping at the altar of Baal, Elijah called God's people to come out saying, "If the Lord be God, then serve Him."

The exodus which Jesus Christ begins in Jerusalem is one which incorporates the deliverance of Moses and Elijah, and a synthesis emerges in which people are freed, cared for, and redeemed, in the full dimensions of their humanity. Christ is the Savior and Healer of both body and soul, individual and corporate life. This synthesis can be seen in the further unfolding of the same story. Peter, James, and John share an experience with Christ in which they hear the voice from heaven saying, "This is my beloved son: hear him." Typically, impetuous Peter says, "Master, it is good for us to be here: let us make three tabernacles; one for you, and one for Moses, and one for Elijah." Peter wanted to stay on the mountaintop with Jesus and forget about the need and hurt and heartache in the valley below.

Meanwhile, in that valley at the foot of the mountain, the remaining nine disciples of Jesus are face-to-face with the world's need epitomized in the life of a seriously ill boy, whose condition is pure agony and hopelessness. His father had brought him to the disciples in the hope that he might be healed. Since Jesus is not present, the disciples, who are moved to compassion, try in their own strength to bring healing to the boy. They fail.

Finally, despite Peter's plea to remain, Jesus strides down the mountain of inspiration into the valley of human need, clothed in the strength of God. And he heals the sick boy. To the dismayed disciples Jesus explains, "This kind can go forth only by prayer and fasting."

We can learn a lesson here. The rejection of Peter's plea to stay on the mountain reminds us that Christians cannot be Christian when they seek to wall themselves off from the world and live on the mountaintop of their own religious experience. Individualistic piety is not enough, for the world waits for our ministry in the agony of the valley. On the other hand, the nine helpless disciples in the valley remind us that the church has no power to heal the world's deep wounds unless it first has been with God on the mountain. The church is never really the church if it is not clothed in the strength and power which comes from a personal relationship with God. But with Christ the church can move through the valley of the world's need and respond to that need. Conversion is never really Christian conversion unless it includes commissioning to a missionary vocation.

This discussion of individualism is neither an attempt to question the importance of an encounter with Christ, nor a claim that Christian conversion is not a deeply and uniquely personal experience. We have held all along that Christian conversion occurs in the lives of individuals, is intensely personal, utterly intimate. But it is never so private as to be solitary. A Christian understanding of conversion would question any attempt to make our experience isolated, sufficient unto itself. Christian conversion would insist that the validity of any encounter with Christ is established by a life of faithfulness. What is needed in the last two decades of the twentieth century is an approach to Christian conversion that lets loose the revolutionary stuff of the Bible on the whole structure of modern society. An understanding of conversion as an individualistic experience without emphasis upon missionary vocation is inadequate in a world crying out for Christian witness in community life, in social justice, in racial honesty, and in financial decency.

When Jesus said to the disciples, "Follow me," they were not invited to leave the world but to walk with Jesus through the world. Now it is true that they were challenged to renounce their false security in the standards and goals of their society, but the divine calling was not away from but through the secular calling; not away from participation, but to worthwhile and redemptive participation.

Third, individualism usually implies a bifurcation of the human being.[18] Earlier we saw how the Bible speaks of Adam as "whole being" *(nefesh)* and affirms that the "whole being" of Adam is created in the image of God. Individualistic interpretations assert that the image of God is only a particular aspect or faculty in Adam's composite being, that instead of "Adam" being understood in biblical terms as the human race, "Adam" means the individual human. Thus, an individualistic interpretation assumes that God breathed into each person a non-material, immortal, rational soul, and it is this soul which comprises a person's essential humanity. If the soul is the essential component of the human, it follows that conversion involves primarily only the soul or spirit. Whatever involvement there is for the total person, it is only inferential involvement, because the main thing is "spiritual" conversion which will assure the continued existence and redemption of an immortal soul.

In this view, then, conversion becomes a private transaction between God and the individual soul and has little or nothing to do with the behavioral or social dimensions of life. Since conversion impacts only the soul and does not involve the total person, other aspects of human nature remain virtually the same. If conversion does not involve the total person, then the fundamental patterns of individual and group relations will remain virtually unaffected by it.

Fourth, individualism normally assumes that the individual is more important than the group. If the relationship between an individual and God is strictly a personal matter, then the church is secondary, merely a collection of individuals created by individuals for their own individual benefit. The church plays only an instrumental role and is in no way considered essential to the salvation of the individual.

It is little wonder, then, that media evangelism and mass evangelism techniques have proved most popular in spreading individualistic religion. These have become the surrogate for genuine Christian community. Whether in a crowd of strangers in a football stadium or in the privacy of one's own home, these settings provide the anonymity and impersonal context for making "decisions" with little risk of accountability to a community of God's people. Moreover, we should not be surprised that these techniques have had minimal success in relating converts to local congregations. In fact, they promote a concept of conversion that militates against genuine involvement in the Body of Christ. These settings have helped to produce what Carl Dudley calls the "new believers," a great host of people who have found a style of religious faith apart from local churches. They emphasize personal freedom, individual decisions, and private religious experiences. For these people faith has become so privatized that the church has become optional equipment.[19] This individualization of Christianity is one of the most disturbing tendencies in our modern world.

The church is the Body of Christ. It is by definition a Body. This

Body took shape in the New Testament world as local churches. Converts were baptized and brought into the fellowship of these congregations. Today, however, the gravitational pull is not in the direction of congregations but more in the direction of some media clientele. People are turning their loyalties more and more toward powerful media personages or celebrities who command huge media empires. It is possible that the church's primary competitor in the final decades of the twentieth century will be a completely private, consumer-oriented religion fostered by the electronic church.

Thomas Luckmann compares modern people to consumers in a supermarket: picking their values by personal choice according to their various social roles and life involvements, and putting them together in a privatized individual myth, which is a shaky support for life because it has no enduring institutional base.[20] People need more than the shaky foundation of our consumer-oriented society. They need the "rock of faith against which the gates of hell shall not prevail," and they need the church of the living God. It is the consistent witness of the Bible that God continues to call out a people, a people who are distinct from the world in their convictions and standards even though they remain immersed in the world.

Now this called-out community of people is central to both the gospel and history. From the day of Pentecost on, the apostles expected converts to join the spirit-filled Body of Christ. Peter's admonition to the people on the day of Pentecost was not only to "turn" and "trust"—as if their conversion could remain an individualistic transaction—but he also summoned them to be baptized and added to the new community of the Spirit (Acts 2:40-47). Incorporation into the church was clearly recognized. We must constantly remind ourselves that historically the Christian faith has always been essentially as much a community concern as a concern of the individual. Norman Kraus contends,

. . . Personal religious experience must be understood as both social and individual, but never as private. We come as individual persons to God, but our relationship to Him can never be exclusive of the brother. Authentic prayer, in which that relationship is expressed, is never "I" centered. It is kingdom centered, always made in the context of the community and its purposes. Every prayer must be addressed to "*our* Father," .... It must be prayed in an attitude of openness to the brother and sister for their good as well as my own. We must always pray as individuals-in-community. To pray "in the name of Christ" is to pray as one who recognizes Christ as head of the body and oneself as a functioning member under his headship.[21]

## EXPERIENTIAL IDOLATRY

Another way to nullify the biblical understanding of conversion is to stereotype a specific kind of *experience* and proclaim that experience as valid and necessary for everyone. This form of tragic, cruel, religious tyranny is becoming increasingly common. A person who has had a rich experience proceeds to invest that *experience* with the status of divinity to which all must give unquestioned acquiescence. Once the pattern of the experience has been given the status of divinity it is beyond critical scrutiny.

Recent converts are especially vulnerable to this temptation. They may tend to canonize and standardize their experience and impose it upon others. And they may have no compunctions about the methods they use. They imply, "If you are converted, you'll be like me! For it will happen to you the way it happened to me!" Now I am not insinuating that young converts are incapable of witness. They are in fact among our most effective evangelists. God uses their witness despite blind spots and clumsiness. All of us have our share of these. I am merely pointing out a subtle danger that those of us who have had dramatic experiences must face, or else we could find ourselves inhibiting the work of God in people's lives.

Unfortunately, we have so succeeded in standardizing the dramatic form of conversion experience that we have muted the impact of the church's witness. The multitudes, whose experiences are not of the dramatic type, have been conditioned to assume that they have nothing to talk about. Inadvertently, we have silenced the huge majority of our people by concentrating exclusively upon the dramatic conversion. Even William James' monumental study, *Varieties of Religious Experience,* has, in some respects, been detrimental. For he tended to deal with persons who had experienced dramatic changes. This is understandable, since the data in such cases are especially conspicuous and easy to contrast. However, Stephen Neill is probably correct in observing that James dealt with instances that were in a way abnormal rather than the more normal type.[22]

Moreover, the use of the Apostle Paul's Damascus Road experience as a prototype for all conversion has had a negative impact upon the church. The ninth chapter of the Book of Acts has been overworked by those who insist that it represents the only genuine type of conversion experience. I am merely observing that it is not the only type that a person may have. This must be stated again and again, for there are many in our churches who are deeply troubled in that they cannot find anything in their past lives that resembles the Damascus Road. Barclay argues that not just anyone can "have the Pauline experience; and to make that experience the standard for conversion is to make the exception the rule." [23] He points out that Paul was out to obliterate Jesus Christ; he was breathing out threat and murder against the church. He wanted to leave the church like a conquered army leaves a scorched earth or a sacked city.

It is clear that the number of men and women in whom that situation is reproduced is infinitesimal. Indifference may have to be broken through; the unawareness of sin may have to be replaced with the searing consciousness of sin; hostility may have to surrender, but this murderous passion of hatred and persecution can hardly at all be paralleled.[24]

Obviously, not every conversion can be a Damascus Road experience. Few Christian converts have been blinded at midday and have heard the risen Lord call out their names in English. Most of the committed Christians I know have met the Lord in a way more akin to the Emmaus Road. While in conversation with a Stranger, they have felt their "hearts burn within them as He opened the Scriptures" (Luke 24:32). Then in the "breaking of bread" or some other sacramental sharing their eyes have been opened, and they have said, "It is true, the Lord has risen!"

Our own personal experience should never be taken as a norm for other people. Each person has a distinctive temperament. Some people are more intuitive, others more logical. Some are more intellectual while others are more emotional. The way God deals with each of us will be marked by the stamp of our own temperament. Barclay says it beautifully: "God has His own secret stairway into every heart." [25] People are infinitely diverse. They not only travel along a variety of roads but they are different within because of various associations with forebears, mothers, fathers, teachers, and peers. Because of this variety we are molded differently. Therefore, we respond differently.

John Wesley understood this. In his admonition to use all the means of grace which God has ordained, he says, "The means into which different men are led and in which they find the blessing of God, are varied, transposed, and combined together, a thousand different ways." [26] There is no one standardized conversion experience, but conversion will be as infinitely varied as human experience itself. And, we can be grateful that God is cracking through our ironclad minds and making the larger biblical understanding of conversion known.

## QUESTIONS FOR THOUGHT AND DISCUSSION

1. The author writes of our allegiance to certain stereotyped forms and formulas of Christian conversion. Describe some of these that you have experienced. What are the limitations of such rigidity (see p. 146)?

2. What does the writer mean by "believism" (p. 148)? How would you contrast believism and faith?

3. Excessive individualism leads to distortions in our understanding and practice of conversion. The author explores four of these. You might try summarizing each.

4. How would you describe the proper relationship in conversion between inward experience and outward expression in the church and the world? As an "evangelist," what can you do to strengthen this relationship?

5. How can you help free others from excessive dependence on one form of conversion experience (e.g., a dramatic form such as Paul's)?

# 10. God's Secret Stairway into Every Heart

The means by which people find the blessing of God are indeed "varied, transposed and combined together a thousand different ways." Since the late 1960s I have been keeping a file drawer labeled "People Who Were Helped." This drawer contains letters from a wide variety of people. Practically all are testimonies of how the grace of God broke in upon their lives in very specific ways. To be honest, I had not opened the file for at least ten years except to enter additional letters. As I thought of Barclay's statement, "God has his own secret stairway into every heart," I remembered that file.

The following letters are characteristic of the infinite variety of ways persons experience Christian conversion. I have omitted names and places in order to protect confidences and have abridged only at the point of eliminating extraneous materials. Otherwise, the letters are quoted verbatim.

A homemaker and mother of four children writes: "I have been a regular church attender all my life; prayed daily and did what I thought was living the Christian life, but felt empty and frustrated. At our church I met several people with an active vital faith. It seemed to radiate. I felt there was more to the Christian life and I started reaching for it. . . . Last Thursday evening I felt terribly troubled and uneasy when I returned home from church. I put a sacred album on our phonograph, Stainer's 'The Crucifixion.' As I listened, I wept. I think this was the first time I had taken Christ personally. It humbled me to think that God would send his Son into the world to die on a cross in order that I might be forgiven. He really must love EVEN ME.

"Again on Friday morning I felt very mixed up and confused, but a friend had given me a book titled *An Adventure in Prayer*. As I was reading, the word *commitment* jumped out at me. It dawned on me that I had never really owned the faith. I had never really committed my life to Christ. Again, I prayed and gave my life to Christ and the most wonderful peace, joy, and love swelled up within me. I felt like I had been released from something. That night at church you served Holy Communion. I felt that a covenant was sealed between God and myself.

"Now I'm starting down a new road. As I look down this road it is as if I'm just beginning to live and I have so much to learn about God. I don't look at the road as a bed of roses. I know there will be problems, discouragements, joys, and sorrows but somehow I know that all of these things can be met, for I am not alone. My problem now is how can I be an effective, growing, serving witness? I'm so new in this business that I wouldn't want to say anything that would hurt Christ's work in others. I want to be a good servant but don't always know how. Nevertheless, I'm happy! You know, the best part of all is that now religion is a joy and not a burden."

A girl who was brought up in a loving Christian home writes the following: "I am thirteen years old and during the worship I got a different look at life. I just can't seem to put it into words, but all I know is it's the most wonderful feeling anyone can have. I almost cried I was so happy. Mom and Dad have taught me that God loves me, but now I really love God. I'm going to try real hard with the help of God to be better. I think now I have the kind of life you were talking about even though I can't explain it. It's hard to say 'thank you' the way you would like to, but I am reserving a place in my heart for you."

The following letter is from a university student who was studying criminal law in anticipation of a career with the Central Intelligence Agency. During two consecutive summers he participated in the Appalachia Service Project, a missionary effort that repairs the houses in the poverty regions of Southern Appalachia. In a lengthy letter he tells how his conversion took place. "The past few weeks have not been enjoyable ones for me, for I have been engaged in a painful conflict, a personal battle deep within me, which I have finally and forever resolved. What is this conflict and why has it manifested itself now? The reasons are numerous, probably the most basic being the environment, its effect on me and my interaction with it.

"To start off, I was raised in a very middle-class, very nice, very normal, very establishment-oriented atmosphere in regard to everything from family and friends to education and politics. But there was a bit of conflict in the area of religion. My father was a faithful church-goer, while my mother was and is as close to being an agnostic as possible without actually being an agnostic in any strict sense of the word. So, although I was baptized and confirmed and attended church regularly, none of these things were done through any initiative on my part. Still, because my mother was a liberal and because she had a large influence on me, religion or lack of a religion became an important personal issue—something which I knew would one day have to be resolved in my own mind. Subsequently I was induced to think dynamically about God and heaven and Christ and the Bible vis-a-vis passively accepting them.

"Throughout high school I considered myself an atheist, at that time the only intelligent thing I could acceptably label myself. Looking back, I was actually an agnostic and remained such until I began college. During that period what might be termed my conversion began. For the first time I was able to see rather than look, and listen rather than hear, and slowly, as I was exposed to various experiences at the university and influenced by sermons, I realized and acknowledged the certainty of the existence of some greater intelligence, some supreme power, call it what you will. This I did without any compromising of myself; and the explanation is really very simple—the stars, the trees, flowers, a blade of grass, a drop of water, a spring breeze or a summer sunset, a child, the love I felt from you.

"After one accepts the existence of an omnipotent entity, that acceptance logically leads to an indestructible, indispensable faith that anything is possible; and so, partly out of the sheer logic of consistency, partly out of a universal fear of death, and partly out of necessity, one cannot help but have faith and hope in some better place, some concept of an afterlife. And, consequently, I do, and it gives meaning and purpose and direction to my life.

"Now, played off against these very mystical, very philosophical, partly existential attitudes about my life are two other dimensions of my personality. One might accurately say that until the present time I have led a very schizophrenic existence: my personality has been a sort of tri-polarization consisting of the troubled philosopher, the socially conscious sympathizer, and the romantically inclined fascist. One must understand that I was unduly influenced by the mass media—television, motion pictures, books—to believe with all of my mind, but none of my heart, that I wanted to work for the Central Intelligence Agency. This is really a difficult thing to admit because it means that I've been living a lie for the last three years, but after hearing a sermon on 'Self-reevaluation' I was motivated to this point. It seems to me that I was born or reborn.

"Now I have always been socially concerned. And yet, I had convinced myself that I wanted to be a spy. In fact, I did such a fantastic job of self-deception that I turned my back on, hid from the problems by which I was most instinctively wrought up. Political raps with fellow students became taboo, marching in any kind of demonstration was unthinkable, giving a damn about anything but my future 'position' with the C.I.A. became a very alien feeling.

"But, something happened, the straw that broke the camel's back. The mass media, which had done such a great job as the catalyst in my self-deception, betrayed itself. It was a newspaper article about the killing of innocent students at Kent State University and how the Justice Department refused to take action though the deaths were ruled 'unnecessary, unwarranted and inexcusable.' After reading *that* I simply said to myself, 'I cannot and will not work within a system which promotes injustice.' So, with my rejection of our government—not our *form* of government, rather the manner in which that delicate and fragile form was being bent and distorted—I came to a crossroads: One fork led to a complete political radicalization of my attitudes towards life in general and, as far as I could surmise, ultimately a deadend; the other led to a complete commitment to a sort of social ministry concerned with people rather than ideologies or ways of governing those people.

"The next question, very logically, was, what institution in contemporary society is the most viable, most effective vehicle to finding a cure for our social life, for ills which must be diagnosed and cured quickly if we are to survive. The law? No. The mass media and journalism? I don't believe so. My answer, not surprisingly, was and remains the church, because if the church, through an Appalachian trip, an innercore ministry, or through a pastor's sermons can reach me, it can and must reach others.

"Thus, I believe in God and I believe in heaven, but what of this Jesus Christ? Well, up until very recently I couldn't believe in people rising from the dead and ascending into heaven or in a human being whom everyone called the Son of God. I couldn't swallow it without compromising myself and all that had been taught to me in school. But I believe I may have found an answer, and somehow this Christ seems very real to me. Could it be that the resurrection and ascension symbolize the existence of the Spirit of Jesus Christ in the world, an undying universal devotion to one's brothers and sisters? And could it be that the resurrection is not just a physical disappearance of Jesus' body from the grave, but a very real reappearance of the proclamation 'to love others as I have loved you. . .' ? If the answer to these questions is yes, well then I have already made the biggest decision of my life: to become a Christian."

The next letter is from an older man who, like the prodigal, had dissipated his life and spent a fortune in riotous living. He writes, "For about two and one-half years I walked under the shadow of a stroke. Twice it raised its head and once in the middle of March it was really bad. I will never forget that morning as I sat in the doctor's office and looked at that report and could not wisecrack: the results of the test were final. Oh, both the doctor and I could have exchanged a few pat phrases, but that morning pat phrases were the last thing I wanted to hear. I wanted to know how in the name of God would I get the pieces picked up. For life suddenly seemed very near and dear to me.

"By some will of fate—maybe you could call it that—a new friend crossed my sky like a comet. He appeared for a while and was gone, but I'll never forget him: a young Methodist minister. I was old enough to be that minister's father. And this is the generation that I had said had nothing, absolutely nothing, to say to me; I didn't even want to be bothered with them. Yet, it was to this generation I turned when the chips were down. In absolute desperation I knocked on this young minister's hotel door late one evening and he welcomed me in. I will never forget those brief moments in that hotel room as long as I live. I guess it was the way he said it to me or maybe it was *what* he said to me. It certainly wasn't what I expected to hear at all and it was far from tea and sympathy. After I blurted my messy story out to him I said, 'How in the name of God did I ever get into this mess and when will all this end? I am miserable, I am lost, I can't sleep. I'll either find life tonight or else I have decided to take my life tonight.'

"The young preacher said, 'Well, it didn't happen over night, did it? It happened a little at a time.' He read the fifteenth chapter of Luke and said I was like a sheep that had nibbled its way lost with its head down; not paying any attention where it was going; just following the path of the greenest grass; eventually to awaken in a wilderness lost and alone. I thought, 'like a sheep'? My father had called me a goose once when I was young, and a young fellow I worked with called me an old goat. Now I was a sheep! But it was true. I had wandered through fields and forests where I had no business going. The preacher said, 'You liked the taste of the grass thinking no one would find out. Now you are sick, broken and tired, and—pardon my saying so—you reak with self-pity.' (That I remember perfectly well.) He said, 'Let's face it, yours is a case of old-fashioned Methodist backsliding. But do you really want to be found by the Shepherd? He's seeking you, you know!' 'Oh yes!' I said, and the two of us knelt beside the bed and I yielded my life to God.

"After discussing this with one of my friends, he said, 'Why didn't you tell your pastor about this? You're a member of that church aren't you?' I said, 'I'll tell you why. I wanted my pastor to go on thinking I was a good little boy who never got his face smeared. I didn't want him to know anything about the dark corners of my life. Now, that's hypocrisy to the Nth degree, but it's the truth.'

"Two nights later I stood near the pulpit of the old church to which I had belonged for years and sang, 'Walk in the light and thou shalt find, thy heart made truly His, who dwells in cloudless light enshrined in whom no darkness is.' I sang, 'Father I stretch my hand to thee, no other help I know, if I would draw myself from thee, whither would I go?' No more backsliding for me!"

A high school senior tells how a small group of Christians within her local church exposed her to the love of God: "It was exactly two years ago that you invited the youth to come to summer sessions with you. I really didn't want to attend, but I agreed to accompany a friend. I'll never forget those preparatory meetings where the church teenagers got to know themselves, each other, and you through contemporary discussions.

"At the end of that summer you breached the big question: 'Would we be interested in going to a work camp in Appalachia?' We said, yes; and that was the beginning of it all. It is impossible for me to pinpoint a day or an hour, but very gradually my life was gripped by a growing assurance that God loved me and forgave me. Looking back on this, it is a mystery to me. I will never understand it, but I know that it is real.

"Our group is a very special organization. The friendships of brothers and sisters under God are so strong and always there when needed. Through this group many have experienced a kind of 'new birth,' but they have experienced much more besides. They have learned management, planning, responsibility, leadership, and, most important of all, how to work with others.

"Each year the group loses some familiar faces as they graduate from high school and gains others as they get old enough to join. I just hope that all the youth realize the immense power and feeling within this group, and that all strive *together* to keep it going. With God's help, I hope this group will always continue to give love and support to all its members as it has to me. It has meant *life* to me!"

A young adult writes about what she calls "a conversion to the world": "This is just a note written so that I can express my gratitude for all that I came to better understand during the New Life Mission. So much that was expressed I had at some time or other thought of, but at the church services and during the Lay Forum I was able to acquire a greater consistency or continuity in my thoughts. Best of all, I realized how very little I know about ministry in the world and how much I need to be 'converted to the world.' I really believe that by God's grace I can be involved in ministry in the world. I now know that I have a role to play, not just something to learn.

"While I was in high school I had the most horrible guilt complex about the fact that I would be attending college someday. That sounds strange, doesn't it? But I couldn't understand how it was quite right to spend four years pampering and cultivating myself so that someday I might have a comfortable and dignified place in society. Afterwards, I attended a church camp and had the opportunity to talk to some very dedicated people in the mission field. I came to understand that to educate myself for myself would be heresy. God gave me a vision of my responsibility in the world. I left that camp with the feeling that someday I would be working in some capacity as a part of the mission of the church.

"In an earlier letter I had expressed the hope that someday you would receive another letter from me and that that letter would express the joy of finding one's place in the kingdom of God. I have found that place!" [The writer goes on to describe her involvement in a remedial reading program for underprivileged students.] "It concerns me that many people seem to have a kind of 'inward conversion,' but I am convinced that the inward conversion without the 'outward conversion to the world' is non-productive as far as the kingdom is concerned."

## GOD WORKS IN MANY WAYS

Even a quick review of these experiences reveals both fundamental similarities and unique differences. I have seen these similarities and differences in every congregation I have served. Some people are members of the church for years without "owning the faith." Joe Hale is correct when he says, "It is possible that there are those who have had all the influences—the Bible, worship, intermingling with Christian people—and yet, it has never come home to them that every individual must make the 'life gamble' of ultimate trust for himself." [1]

In E. Stanley Jones's famous book, *Conversion*, he describes three categories of people who are present in every congregation. He speaks of these categories in terms of three circles. There is an inner circle of those who have a vital faith in God. This basic trust in God impacts their whole life and is a constant source of purpose, strength, and inspiration. The second circle is comprised of people who have a "secondhand faith." They have been influenced by the religion of their parents, the customs that have been handed down, but they have never really committed themselves to the living God. The third circle is comprised of a group who attach themselves to a local church because they believe it will enhance their status in the community and increase their business contacts. These are the C.P.E.'s—the Christmas, Palm Sunday, and Easter attenders. They make annual or semi-annual pilgrimages to the church. [2]

Bruce Reed gives two additional categories of persons who are members of this third circle. One group is that which engages in "representative oscillation." These persons seldom or never attend worship, but it is important for them that a member of their family or an acquaintance or a significant person in the community attends. It is as if such a person were attending on their behalf. They even become anxious if this person does not attend. In addition, there are those who engage in "vicarious oscillation." Members of this group do not identify themselves with any particular individual worshiper, but it is important that the church building remain in the community. They need to hear church bells ringing and they need to see people going to church. They may be members of a congregation, but the church is a place to stay away from. Nevertheless, it would be upsetting to them if anyone should suggest that the church be removed from the community. [3]

Some people in Jones's second and third circles would fit into the stage or category that John Westerhoff calls "affiliative faith." They really need to participate in the church's activities and they do so wholeheartedly, but they get stymied at the affiliative stage, as important as it is, and fail to move on to "an owned style of faith." Because of this failure the conversion process is thwarted.[4] However, after much questing and struggle, many of these persons do come to "own the faith."

Some have been members of the church in name only. Their name is on the membership book, but the faith has little if any meaning. As a matter of fact, their life is in no way impacted by the lordship of Jesus Christ.

Others might have known a vital relationship with God in the past but not any longer. They live their life in selfishness and indulge themselves to the point of debauchery. Then, as a result of some radical change or crisis, they see their emptiness and seek God with a whole heart.

Still others fight an intellectual battle that involves not only doubt regarding basic theological formulations but existential doubt regarding the meaning of life and the possibility of the world's future. Sometimes these persons are motivated by the deep needs of others. If the church can provide programs that will afford them the opportunity of first-hand involvement in people's pains and in ameliorating society's structures, these activities often drive them to questions of ultimate concern.[5] It has been my privilege to witness numerous conversions that fit this pattern, and I hope that the church will give increasing importance to this model. It is a bonafide model for evangelism that has been given only minimal attention, especially in the evangelical community.

Some have come to faith as a result of involvement in small koinonia groups where they felt loved, accepted, affirmed, and challenged. They may not be able to pinpoint the day or the hour, but the assurance of God's grace is very real to them and their lives bear fruit of that assurance.

Still others discover God as children, children who have been fortunate enough to witness the love of God in the lives of committed parents and a faithful congregation. They were incorporated into the church by baptism as infants. The conversion process unfolds for them as they mature. Eventually, the children begin to walk on their own feet and accept for themselves the accepting love of God. This often happens in the rite of confirmation.

My father and mother were converted through the ministry of a compassionate pastor who persistently loved them and pursued them until they were willing to open their lives to the gospel. I began my Christian pilgrimage in a very simple way. I trusted my father. I had no reason to distrust him, and I could see that what was happening to him on the night of his conversion had the profoundest meaning and was infinitely important. When he asked me to go to the altar, I did so. I suppose one could say that the threshold of my own pilgrimage was initiated by response to an authority figure in whom I had trust. But, when I went forward I discovered so much more besides. I actually began a journey in the grace of God, a journey that continues to enliven my spirit, excite my mind, fill my heart with hope and evoke my best efforts in God's kingdom. This humble beginning opened for me the possibility of a new life in a new community. It started me on a road that lures me forward with visions of a new heaven and a new earth.

The point of all this has been to show that God has a secret stairway into every heart, that is, God works in many different ways in order to communicate the gospel and bring people to faith. Conversion happens to different people in different ways and on different levels, and it is more than a static, once-in-a-lifetime experience. Rather it is a dynamic force of change in terms of both our individual lives and the society of which we are a part. To stereotype a certain model, experience, process, or order as the "only way" constitutes a serious perversion of the biblical perspective and it puts a tragic limitation on the scope of the gospel's power.

Notice, I said that conversion happens to different people on different levels. D. T. Niles makes this clear when he says, "The object of evangelism is conversion, conversion to Christ and personal discipleship to him. But involved also in this conversion are conversion to the Christian community and conversion to Christian ideas and ideals. All three conversions must take place even

though the order in which they take place may be different. . . ."
Niles concludes, "It is futile and perverse to isolate these three
movements of the soul from one another and treat them in opposi-
tion to one another. They belong together, each makes the others
possible, and they derive meaning from one another." [6]

The order in which these conversions take place shows
tremendous diversity. For some the first conversion is largely to
the Christian community. For others conversion to Christian
ideas and ideals comes first and is followed by conversion to
Christ and the Christian community. For others it is conversion
to Christ and personal discipleship which is followed by conversion to the Christian community.

All of these levels or stages or elements are intrinsic to the total
fact of conversion, but there is no fixed rule of antecedence and
consequence. No matter what the order, conversion is a radical
transformation after which follows, on all levels of life, an inter-
locking series of changes and developments. A changed relationship with God brings changes that are personal, social, moral,
and intellectual. The converted person relates, performs, values,
and apprehends differently because the converted person has become different. To put it in Paul's words, "If anyone is in Christ,
he is a new creation; the old has passed away, behold, the new has
come" (2 Cor. 5:17, RSV).

In many ways Christian conversion is as mysterious as the
wind. We cannot know everything about it, but we can know
enough. Because conversion comes as a result of the work of the
divine Spirit we cannot stereotype it. "The Spirit blows where it
wills." The Spirit works in many different ways. But let no one
say that because conversion cannot be stereotyped it need not
happen at all. That is sheer nonsense! How it happens shows wide
diversity, but that it must happen is singularly important. There
is no substitute for Christian conversion.

## QUESTIONS FOR THOUGHT AND DISCUSSION

1. In the six accounts of conversion quoted in this chapter,
what similarities do you find? What differences?

2. How well do E. Stanley Jones's three circles of members (p. 168) fit your congregation? Would you describe them differently or add other categories? What does this imply for conversion in your church?

3. In summary, how has this book influenced your thought on conversion? What eight or ten major concepts or themes stand out?

4. How will this book now influence your behavior? In your ministry with others, what will you do differently?

# Notes

## Introduction: In the Beginning

1. Keith Miller, *The Becomers* (Waco, Texas: Word Books, 1973), pp. 132–133.
2. Edward Schillebeeckx, *Christ* (New York: Seabury Press, 1980), pp. 32, 34.

## 1. Christian Conversion in Theological Perspective

1. H. H. Farmer, *The Word of Reconciliation* (Nashville: Abingdon Press, 1966), p. 71.
2. Leander Keck, "The God of the Gospel" (an unpublished manuscript).
3. Leander Keck, *A Future for the Historical Jesus* (Nashville: Abingdon Press, 1971), pp. 100–106.
4. Bruce Reed, *The Dynamics of Religion* (London: Darton, Longmann & Todd, 1978), pp. 210–211.
5. Keck, "The God of the Gospel."

## 2. The Modern Babel

1. Jacques Ellul, *The Technological Society* (New York: Vintage Books, Random House, Inc., 1967), pp. 428–429.
2. John Westerhoff III, *Will Our Children Have Faith?* (New York: Seabury Press, 1976), p. 92.
3. John E. Biersdorf, *Hunger for Experience* (New York: Seabury Press, 1975), p. 4.

4. Ibid., p. 11.
5. Ibid., p. 21.
6. Ibid., p. 24.
7. Ibid., p. 106.
8. Peter L. Berger, *The Heretical Imperative* (New York: Doubleday, 1979), p. 188.
9. Ibid., p. 9.
10. Joe Hale, "The Future History of American Methodism" (an unpublished manuscript).
11. Paul Tournier, *The Person Reborn* (London: S.C.M. Press, Ltd., 1966), p. 101.
12. Professor Paul Kurtz, an interview, in "Some People Believe Anything They See on T.V.," *U.S. News and World Report,* May 21, 1979, pp. 52–54.
13. *Saturday Evening Post,* Vol. 251, No. 3 (April 1979), p. 34.
14. Ibid., p. 136.
15. Thomas Merton, "Final Integration" in *Conversion,* ed. Walter E. Conn (New York: Alba House, 1978), p. 271.
16. See Jacques Ellul, *Propaganda: The Formation of Man's Attitudes* (New York: Vintage Press, 1973).
17. See John E. Smith, "The Concept of Conversion" in *Conversion,* ed. Walter E. Conn (New York: Alba House, 1978), pp. 51–61.
18. The Bangkok Assembly, *Culture and Identity,* 1973, p. 75.
19. William Sargant, *Battle for the Mind* (Garden City, New York: Doubleday and Co., Inc., 1957), pp. 102–105.
20. Arthur Koestler, *The God That Failed,* ed. Richard Crossman (New York: Harper Brothers, 1949), p. 23.
21. Sargant, *Battle for the Mind,* p. 105.
22. William James, *The Varieties of Religious Experience* (New York: Mentor Press, 1958), pp. 41, 157.
23. For a critique of James' approach see Wayne E. Oates, "Conversion: Sacred and Secular" in *Conversion,* ed. Walter E. Conn (New York: Alba House, 1978).
24. George E. Sweazey, *The Church as Evangelist* (New York: Harper & Row, 1978), pp. 113–114.
25. Lewis R. Rambo, "Psychological Perspectives on Conversion,"

*Pacific Theological Review*, Vol. XIII, No. 2 (Spring 1980) p. 22.

26. Ibid., p. 21.
27. Quoted by Phillip Potter in his address to the Central Committee in Crete, *W.C.C. Central Committee Minutes, 1960,* August, 1967, p. 214.
28. John R. W. Stott, *Christian Mission in the Modern World* (Downer's Grove, Illinois: I.V.P., 1975), pp. 109–112.
29. William Barclay, *Turning to God* (Grand Rapids, Michigan: Baker Bookhouse, 1973), pp. 90–100.
30. J. G. Davies, *Dialogue with the World* (London: S.C.M. Press, 1967, p. 54.
31. Karl Barth, "The Awakening to Conversion" in *Conversion,* ed. Walter E. Conn (New York: Alba House, 1978), p. 36.
32. Bryan Green, *The Practice of Evangelism* (New York: Charles Scribner's Sons, 1951), p. 16.
33. Schillebeeckx, *Christ*, p. 20.
34. Paul Löffler, "The Biblical Concept of Conversion" in *Mission Trends, No. 2*, ed. Gerald H. Anderson & Thomas F. Stransky (Grand Rapids: William B. Eerdmans Publishing Co., 1975), p. 42.

## 3. The Biblical Meaning of Conversion

1. Paul Tillich, *Systematic Theology, Vol. III* (Chicago: The University of Chicago Press, 1963), p. 219.
2. See *Theological Dictionary of the New Testament,* ed. Gerhard Friedrich (Grand Rapids, Mich.: Eerdmans Publishing Co., 1975), pp. 714–729.
3. Smith, "The Concept of Conversion" in *Conversion*, p. 51.
4. See William L. Holladay, *The Concise Hebrew and Aramaic Lexicon of the Old Testament* (Grand Rapids, Mich: Eerdmans Publishing Co., 1971), pp. 362–369.
5. Tillich, *Systematic Theology, III*, p. 219.
6. Löffler, "Biblical Concept" in *Mission Trends,* No. 2, p. 30.
7. *Theological Dictionary of the New Testament,* ed. Friedrich, p. 723.

8. Barclay, *Turning to God,* pp. 24, 25.
9. Ibid., p. 19.
10. *Theological Dictionary of the New Testament,* ed. Friedrich, p. 726.
11. Barclay, *Turning to God,* pp. 21–22.
12. Norman Kraus, *The Authentic Witness* (Grand Rapids, Mich.: Eerdmans Publishing Co., 1979), pp. 124–127.
13. Hendrikus Berkhof, *Christian Faith* (Grand Rapids, Mich.: Eerdmans Publishing Co., 1979), pp. 429, 430.
14. Hans Küng, "Conversion" in *Conversion,* ed. Walter E. Conn (New York: Alba House, 1978), pp. 273–274.
15. Barclay, *Turning to God,* p. 26.
16. Charles Edwin Carlston, "Metanoeo and Church Discipline" (unpublished Ph.D. thesis, Harvard University, 1959), p. 141.
17. Erik Routley, *Conversion* (Philadelphia: Fortress Press, 1960), p. 7.
18. Hans Küng, "What Is the Christian Message?" in *Mission Trends, No. 1,* ed. Gerald H. Anderson and Thomas F. Stransky (New York: Paulist Press, 1974), p. 102.
19. Orlando E. Costas, "Conversion as a Complex Experience" in *Down to Earth,* ed. John R. W. Stott and Robert Coote (Grand Rapids, Michigan: Eerdmans Publishing Co., 1980), p. 184.
20. Löffler, "Biblical Concept" in *Mission Trends, No. 2,* p. 40.
21. Gabriel Fackre, *Word in Deed* (Grand Rapids, Michigan: Eerdmans Publishing Co., 1975), pp. 81–82.

## 4. Conversion Is God's Idea

1. Gabriel Fackre, *The Christian Story* (Grand Rapids, Michigan: Eerdmans Publishing Co., 1978), p. 233.
2. Karl Barth, *The Humanity of God,* translated by John Newton Thomas (Richmond: John Knox Press, 1960), pp. 45–46.
3. Jürgen Moltmann, *The Church in the Power of the Spirit* (New York: Harper and Row Publishers, 1977), p. 62.
4. Brian Mahan, "Toward Fire and Light: The Faith of Blaise Pascal" in *Trajectories in Faith,* ed. James W. Fowler and

Robin W. Lovin (Nashville: Abingdon Press, 1980), pp. 111–112.

5. *The United Methodist Book of Hymns*, p. 96.
6. Moltmann, *Church in Power of Spirit*, pp. 53–55.
7. Ibid., p. 56.
8. Karl Barth, *Church Dogmatics*, Vol. II (Edinburgh: T. and T. Clark, 1955), p. 359.
9. Tillich, *Systematic Theology, III,* pp. 112–113.
10. *A Theological Word Book of the Bible,* ed. Allan Richardson (New York: The Macmillan Co., 1950), p. 132.
11. Hans Küng, *Does God Exist?*, trans. by Edward Quinn (New York: Doubleday and Co., 1980), p. 690.
12. Ibid.
13. Tillich, *Systematic Theology, III*, p. 138.
14. Fackre, *Christian Story*, p. 220.
15. Barclay, *Turning to God*, pp. 29–30.
16. John Wesley, "An Earnest Appeal to Men of Reason and Religion" in *John Wesley,* ed. Albert Outler (New York: Oxford University Press, 1964), p. 385.
17. John Wesley, "The Law Established by Faith: Discourse II" in *John Wesley,* ed. Albert Outler (New York: Oxford University Press, 1964), pp. 226–227.
18. *John Wesley*, ed. Outler, p. 232.
19. Roland H. Bainton, *Here I Stand* (New York: A Mentor Book, 1950), pp. 49–50.
20. Reuel L. Howe, *Man's Need and God's Action* (Greenwich, Connecticut: Seabury Press, 1953), p. 22.
21. H. H. Farmer, *The Servant of the Word* (Philadelphia: Fortress Press, 1942), pp. 22–24.
22. Albert C. Outler, *Theology in the Wesleyan Spirit* (Nashville: Tidings, 1975), pp. 12–13.
23. Samuel Shoemaker, *How to Become a Christian* (New York: Harper and Row, 1953), p. 67.
24. A. Skevington Wood, *The Burning Heart* (Minneapolis, Minnesota: Bethany Fellowship Inc., 1978), pp. 161–162.
25. Outler, *Theology,* p. 85.
26. E. Stanley Jones, *Conversion* (New York: Abingdon Press, 1959), p. 37.

27. Ibid.
28. Robert G. Tuttle, *John Wesley* (Grand Rapids, Michigan: Zondervan Publishing House, 1978), p. 77.
29. *John Wesley*, ed. Outler, p. 61.
30. Ibid., p. 65.

## 5. The Good News of Salvation

1. Theodore Runyon, "What About Those . . . ?" (an unpublished manuscript).
2. Barth, "Awakening" in *Conversion*, pp. 48–49.
3. D. T. Niles, *That They May Have Life* (New York: Harper and Brothers, 1951), p. 18.
4. Runyon, "What About Those . . . ?"
5. Emil Brunner, *Truth as Encounter* (Philadelphia: Westminster Press, 1964), p. 114.
6. Ibid., p. 49.
7. Moltmann, *Church in Power of Spirit*, p. 77.
8. Ibid., p. 208.
9. Dietrich Bonhoeffer, *The Cost of Discipleship* (New York: The Macmillan Company, 1961), p. 225.
10. Thomas L. Torrance, "The Word of God and the Response of Man" in *Theological Foundations for Ministry*, ed. Ray S. Anderson (Grand Rapids, Michigan: Eerdmans Publishing Co., 1979), p. 115.
12. Moltmann, *Church in Power of Spirit*, p. 82.
13. James I. Packer, "The Gospel: Its Content and Communication" in *Down to Earth*, ed. Stott and Coote (Grand Rapids: Eerdmans, 1980), p. 101.
14. Fackre, *Christian Story*, p. 15.
15. James C. Logan, "The Roots of Our Social Vision" in *engage/social action* (December 1979), p. 36.
16. Fackre, *Christian Story*, p. 72.
17. Ibid., p. 16.
18. Fackre, *Word in Deed*, p. 38.
19. Fackre, *Christian Story*, pp. 145–146.
20. Logan, "Roots of Social Vision" in *Social Action*, p. 27.

21. Barth, "Awakening to Conversion" in *Conversion*, p. 48.
22. Leander Keck, "Theological Themes in Romans" (an unpublished manuscript).
23. Moltmann, *Church in Power of Spirit*, p. 206.
24. See L. Harold DeWolf, *A Theology of the Living Church* (New York: Harper and Brothers, 1953), pp. 287–296.

## 6. Who Needs Conversion and Why?

1. Karl Barth, *Church Dogmatics*, ed. G. W. Bromiley and T. F. Torrance (Edinburgh: T. and T. Clark, 1956), Vol. 4, Part 1, pp. 358–397: Part 2, pp. 378–388.
2. Merton, "Integration" in *Conversion*, p. 267.
3. Helmut Thielicke, "The Evangelical Faith" in *Theological Foundations for Ministry*, ed. Ray S. Anderson (Edinburg: T. and T. Clark Ltd., 1979), p. 90.
4. See George Morris, *Shalom* (Nashville: Tidings, 1974), pp. 35–53.
5. St. Augustine, *The Confessions*, Book I (New York: Pocket Books Inc., 1957), p. 1.
6. Paul Tillich, *Systematic Theology, Vol. II* (Chicago: University of Chicago Press, 1957), pp. 44–59.
7. George Buttrick, *Christ and Man's Dilemma* (Nashville: Abingdon-Cokesbury Press, 1946), pp. 26–29.
8. *Luther's Works*, Vol. VI (Philadelphia: Muhlenberg Press, 1932), p. 450.
9. Tillich, *Systematic Theology, II*, p. 56.
10. Outler, *Theology*, p. 34.
11. Ibid., p. 38.
12. Ibid., p. 37.
13. *Cur Deus Homo*, I, 21.
14. Colin Morris, "The Word Became Flesh" in *Proceedings of the Thirteenth World Methodist Conference*, ed. Joe Hale (Waynesville, N.C.: Mountaineer Press, 1977), p. 192.
15. Schillebeeckx, *Christ*, p. 744.
16. See C. Norman Kraus, *The Authentic Witness* (Grand Rapids, MI: Eerdmans, 1979).

17. Gene M. Tucker, "The Creation and Fall: A Reconsideration" in *Lexington Theological Quarterly*, Vol. XIII, No. 4, October, 1978, p. 115.
18. Kraus, *Authentic Witness*, p. 112.
19. Berkhof, *Christian Faith*, p. 208.
20. Ibid., pp. 208–209.
21. Outler, *Theology*, pp. 41–42.
22. William Temple, *Christianity and Social Order* (London: S.C.M. Press Edition, 1950), pp. 36–37.
23. See Raymond Fung's excellent article: "Evangelism Today" in *A Monthly Letter about Evangelism*, The World Council of Churches, Nos. 7/8 (July-August 1979).
24. For an excellent discussion of this point see: Leander Keck, "Evangelism in Theological Perspective" in *Evangelism: Mandates for Action*, ed. James T. Laney (New York: Hawthorne Books, Inc., 1975), pp. 34–68.
25. Westerhoff, *Children Have Faith*, pp. 35–36.

## 7. Christian Conversion: Facets of the Process (Part One)

1. Colin W. Williams, *John Wesley's Theology Today* (Nashville: Abingdon, 1960), p. 41.
2. F. Gerald Ensley, *Persons Can Change* (Nashville: Graded Press, 1963), p. 31.
3. Ibid., p. 37.
4. Barclay, *Turning to God,* pp. 11–12.
5. Albert Outler, *Evangelism in the Wesleyan Spirit* (Nashville: Tidings, 1971), pp. 43–44.
6. Ibid., pp. 44–45.
7. Ibid., p. 45.
8. See George Morris, *Shalom* (Nashville: Tidings, 1974), p. 41.
9. P. T. Forsyth, *The Principle of Authority*, Second Edition (London, 1952), pp. 186ff.
10. Outler, *Evangelism*, p. 43.
11. Charles V. Gerkin, *Crisis Experience in Modern Life* (Nashville: Abingdon Press, 1979), p. 32.
12. Oates, "Conversion" in *Conversion*, p. 152.

13. Paul E. Johnson, "Conversion" in *Conversion*, ed. Walter E. Conn (New York: Alba House, 1978), p. 176.
14. Jacques Pasquier, "Experience in Conversion" in *Conversion*, p. 198.
15. Urban T. Holmes III and John H. Westerhoff III, *Christian Believing* (New York: Seabury Press, 1979), p. 35.
16. Miller, *Becomers*, pp. 121–122.
17. Jonathan Edwards, *A Faithful Narrative of the Surprising Work of God* (Grand Rapids, Michigan: Baker Bookhouse, 1979 reprint), p. 36.
18. *John Wesley*, ed. Outler, p. 33.
19. John Wesley, *Works*, Vol. 6 (Grand Rapids, Michigan: Zondervan, 1973), p. 509.
20. Wesley, "The Fullness of Faith" in *John Wesley*, ed. Outler, p. 273.
21. John Wesley, "Spirit of Bondage and Adoption," Sermon IX, *Standard Sermons*, Part I (Salem, Ohio: Schmul Publishers, 1967 reprint), p. 89.
22. Tillich, *Systematic Theology, III*, p. 223.
23. Routley, *Conversion*, p. 28.
24. *Works,* Vol. 6, p. 515.
25. John Wesley, "Justification by Faith" in *John Wesley*, ed. Outler, pp. 202–203.
26. John Wesley, "Ye Are Saved Through Faith" in *John Wesley*, ed. Outler, p. 273.
27. *Sanctification and Liberation*, ed. Theodore Runyon (Nashville: Abingdon, 1981), pp. 32–33.
28. Leander E. Keck, *Mandate to Witness* (Chicago: Judson Press, 1964), p. 45.
29. *Book of Hymns*, p. 137.

## 8. Christian Conversion: Facets of the Process (Part Two)

1. Outler, *Evangelism*, p. 38.
2. See John R. Hendrick, *Opening the Door of Faith* (Atlanta: John Knox Press, 1977) for an excellent treatment of the nature of faith.

3. John Wesley, "Of True Christian Faith" in *John Wesley*, ed. Albert C. Outler, p. 129.

4. John Wesley, "Doctrinal Summaries" in *John Wesley*, ed. Albert C. Outler, p. 189.

5. John Wesley, "An Earnest Appeal to Men of Reason and Religion" in *John Wesley*, ed. Albert C. Outler, p. 404.

6. Paul Scherer, *The Word God Sent* (New York: Harper and Row, 1965), p. 6.

7. John Wesley, "Justification by Faith" in *John Wesley*, ed. Albert C. Outler, p. 205.

8. For an excellent treatment of faith as trust see: Leander E. Keck, *A Future for the Historical Jesus* (Nashville: Abingdon Press, 1971), p. 67 ff.

9. John Wesley, "Marks of the New Birth" in *Wesley's Doctrinal Standards*, Part I, ed. N. Burwash (Salem, Ohio: Schmul Publishers, 1967 reprint), p. 174.

10. Costas, "Conversion" in *Down to Earth*, ed. Stott and Coote, p. 182.

11. Keck, *Historical Jesus*, p. 185.

12. Küng, "Christian Conversion" in *Conversion*, ed. Walter E. Conn, p. 274.

13. *John Wesley*, ed. Albert C. Outler (New York: Oxford University Press, 1964), pp. 53–54.

14. Joe Hale, *Design for Evangelism* (Nashville: Tidings, 1969), pp. 25–30 (edited).

15. *Wesley's Standard Sermons*, Vol. I, ed. Edward H. Sugden (London: The Epworth Press, 1955), p. 299n.

16. See George Morris, *Shalom* (Nashville: Tidings, 1974), pp. 48–49.

17. David C. Steinmetz, "Reformation and Conversion" in *Theology Today*, Vol. XXV, No. 1 (April 1978), p. 30.

18. Bonhoeffer, *Discipleship*, pp. 35–36.

19. See Fackre, *Christian Story*, pp. 98ff; 147ff; 189ff.

20. *Sanctification*, ed. Theodore Runyon, p. 10.

21. *Wesley's Standard Sermons*, ed. Edward Sugden, p. 120.

22. John Wesley, "The Great Privilege of Those That Are Born of God," *Works*, Vol. V (Grand Rapids, MI: Zondervan), pp. 223–224.

23. John Wesley, "On God's Vineyard" in *John Wesley,* ed. Outler, p. 108.
24. John Wesley, "Ye Are Saved Through Faith" in *John Wesley,* ed. Albert Outler, p. 274.
25. John Wesley, "Repentance of Believers," *Wesley's Standard Sermons,* ed. Sugden, Vol. II. p. 380.
26. Ibid., p. 240.
27. John Wesley, "Justification by Faith" in *John Wesley,* ed. Outler, p. 200.
28. *Sanctification,* ed. Theodore Runyon, p. 39.
29. Ibid., pp. 36-37.
30. John Wesley, *Works,* Vol. IV, pp. 46–47.
31. *Sanctification,* ed. Theodore Runyon, p. 46.
32. Leslie Newbigin, *The Finality of Christ* (London: SCM Press, 1969), pp. 93, 96, 98.
33. Gabriel Fackre, "Conversion," *Andover Newton Quarterly,* Vol. XIV, No. 3 (January 1974), pp. 181–182.
34. Moltmann, *Church in Power of Spirit,* p. 80.
35. Dietrich Bonhoeffer, *Life Together* (New York: Harper & Row, 1954), p. 23.
36. Jones, *Conversion,* p. 39.
37. John Baillie, *Invitation to Pilgrimage* (London: Oxford University Press, 1942), p. 119.
38. See Carl S. Dudley, *Where Have All Our People Gone?* (New York: Pilgrim Press, 1979).
39. Ibid., p. 21.
40. John Wesley, *Works,* Vol. V, pp. 296, 302.
41. Löffler, "Conversion" in *Mission Trends, No. 2,* p. 42.
42. Barclay, *Turning to God,* pp. 102–103.
43. Kraus, *Witness,* p. 92.
44. Ibid.
45. For those interested in pursuing the subject in greater depth, I would recommend: John Baillie, *Baptism and Conversion* (New York: Charles Scribner's Sons, 1963); Lorna Brockett, *The Theology of Baptism* (Hale's Corner, Wisconsin: Clergy Book Service, 1971); Reginald H. Fuller, "Christian Initiation in the New Testament" in *Made, Not Born* (Notre Dame: University of Notre Dame Press, 1976); Joachim Jeremias,

*Infant Baptism in the First Four Centuries* (London: S.C.M. Press, 1960); Joachim Jeremias, *The Origins of Infant Baptism* (Naperville, Illinois: Alec R. Allenson, Inc., 1963); Aidan Kavanagh, *The Shape of Baptism* (Pueblo Press, 1979); Geoffrey Wainwright, *Christian Initiation* (London: Lutterworth Press, 1969).

46. Michael Green, *Evangelism in the Early Church* (Grand Rapids, MI: Eerdmans, 1970), p. 153.
47. Westerhoff, *Children Have Faith,* pp. 89–103.

## 9. Inhibitors to Christian Conversion

1. José Míguez Bonino, Wesley's Doctrine of Sanctification from a Liberationist's Perspective" in *Sanctification and Liberation,* ed. Theodore Runyon (Nashville: Abingdon Press, 1981), p. 56.
2. Edwards, *Narrative,* pp. 64–65.
3. Ibid., p. 38.
4. Samuel Southard, *Pastoral Evangelism* (Nashville: Broadman Press, 1962), pp. 29–30.
5. Hendrick, *Opening the Door to Faith,* pp. 16–17.
6. Routley, *Conversion,* p. 46.
7. As quoted in Hans Küng, *Justification* (New York: Thomas Nelson and Sons Press, 1964), p. 70.
8. Fackre, *Word in Deed,* p. 104.
9. Donald A. McGavran and Winfield C. Arn, *Ten Steps for Church Growth* (New York: Harper & Row, 1977), pp. 52–53, 88.
10. *Interpreter's Bible,* 12 Vol. Commentary, Editor George A. Buttrick (New York: Abingdon Press, Vol. VIII), p. 779.
11. Barth, "Awakening" in *Conversion,* p. 35.
12. Virginia S. Thatcher, *The New Webster Encyclopedic Dictionary of the English Language* (Chicago: Consolidated Book Publishers, 1962), p. 437.
13. Barclay, *Turning to God,* p. 102.
14. Steven C. Neill, "Conversion" in *Focus on Evangelism,* ed.

George Hunter (Nashville: Discipleship Resources, 1978), p. 47.

15. *The Christian Century,* Vol. XCVII, No. 37 (November 19, 1980), p. 1121.
16. Robert H. Thouless, "The Psychology of Conversion" in *Conversion,* ed. Walter E. Conn (New York: Alba House, 1978), p. 141.
27. I am indebted to my friend, John Nichol, for this treatment of the transfiguration.
28. See Norman Kraus, *The Authentic Witness* (Grand Rapids, MI: Eerdmans Publishing Co., 1979).
19. Dudley, *People Gone,* pp. 30, 116.
20. Thomas Luckmann, *Invisible Religion* (New York: Macmillan Publishing Co., 1967), pp. 97, 99.
21. Kraus, *Witness,* p. 113.
22. Neill, "Conversion," p. 40.
23. Barclay, *Turning to God,* p. 93.
24. Ibid.
25. Ibid.
26. John Wesley, "The Means of Grace," Sermon XVI, in *Wesley's Doctrinal Standards,* Part I, ed. Rev. N. Burwash (Salem, Ohio: Schmul Publishers, 1881), p. 161.

**10. God's Secret Stairway into Every Heart**

1. Hale, *Design,* p. 31.
2. Jones, *Conversion,* pp. 9–12.
3. Reed, *Dynamics,* pp. 54–56.
4. Westerhoff, *Children Have Faith,* pp. 94–98.
5. For the best discussion of this process, see: George Hunter's "Inductive Mission Model" in *The Contagious Congregation* (Nashville: Abingdon Press, 1979), pp. 48–59.
6. Niles, *Life,* pp. 82–83.

# Bibliography

Anderson, Gerald H., and Stransky, Thomas F., Editors. *Mission Trends No. 1*. New York: Paulist Press and Eerdmans Publishing Co., 1974.

_____, Editors. *Mission Trends No. 2*. New York: Paulist Press and Eerdmans Publishing Co., 1975.

Anderson, Ray S., Editor. *Theological Foundations for Ministry*. Grand Rapids, Michigan: Eerdmans Publishing Co., 1979.

Armstrong, Richard Stoll. *Service Evangelism*. Philadelphia: Westminster Press, 1979.

Arn, Winfield C., and McGavran, Donald A. *Ten Steps for Church Growth*. New York: Harper & Row, 1977.

Augustine, St. *The Confessions*. Book I. New York: Pocket Books Inc., 1957.

Baillie, John. *Invitation to Pilgrimage*. London: Oxford University Press, 1942.

_____. *Baptism and Conversion*. New York: Charles Scribner's Sons, 1963.

Bainton, Roland H. *Here I Stand*. New York: A Mentor Book, 1950.

The Bangkok Assembly. *Culture and Identity*. Bangkok, 1973.

Barclay, William. *Turning to God*. Grand Rapids, Michigan: Baker Bookhouse, 1973.

Barth, Karl. *Church Dogmatics*. Vols. I–V, General Editors, G. W. Bromiley and T. F. Torrance. Various Translators. Edinburgh: T. & T. Clark, 1936–1962.

_____. *The Humanity of God*. Translated by Thomas Weiser and John N. Thomas. Richmond: John Knox Press, 1960.

Berger, Peter L. *The Heretical Imperative*. New York: Doubleday, 1979.

Berkhof, Hendrikus. *Christian Faith*. Grand Rapids, Michigan: Eerdmans Publishing Co., 1979.

Biersdorf, John E. *Hunger for Experience*. New York: Seabury Press, 1975.

Bonhoeffer, Dietrich. *The Cost of Discipleship*. New York: Macmillan Co., 1959.

_____. *Life Together*. New York: Harper & Row, 1954.

Brockett, Lorna. *The Theology of Baptism*. Hale's Corner, Wisconsin: Clergy Book Service, 1971.

Brunner, Emil. *Truth as Encounter*. Philadelphia: Westminster Press, 1964.

Buttrick, George. *Christ and Man's Dilemma*. Nashville: Abingdon-Cokesbury Press, 1946.

Carlston, Charles Edwin. *Metanoeo and Church Discipline*. Unpublished Ph.D. dissertation, Harvard University, 1959.

Conn, Walter E., Editor. *Conversion.* New York: Alba House, 1978.

Coote, Robert, and Stott, John R. W., Editors. *Down to Earth.* Grand Rapids, Michigan: Eerdmans Publishing Co., 1980.

Davies, J. G. *Dialogue with the World.* London: S.C.M. Press, 1967.

De Jong, Pieter. *Evangelism and Contemporary Theology.* Nashville: Tidings, 1962.

DeWolf, Harold L. *A Theology of the Living Church.* New York: Harper and Brothers, 1953.

Dudley, Carl S. *Where Have All Our People Gone?* New York: Pilgrim Press, 1979.

Edwards, Jonathan. *A Faithful Narrative of the Surprising Work of God.* Grand Rapids, Michigan: Baker Bookhouse, 1979 reprint.

Ellul, Jacques. *Propaganda: The Formation of Man's Attitudes.* New York: Vintage Press, 1973.

————. *The Technological Society.* New York: Vintage Books, Random House, Inc., 1967.

Ensley, F. Gerald. *Persons Can Change.* Nashville: Graded Press, 1963.

Fackre, Gabriel. *The Christian Story.* Grand Rapids, Michigan: Eerdmans Publishing Co., 1978.

————. "Conversion." *Andover Newton Quarterly* 14 (January 1974), pp. 171–189.

_____. *Do and Tell: Engagement Evangelism in the '70s*. Grand Rapids, Michigan: Eerdmans Publishing Co., 1973.

_____. *Word in Deed*. Grand Rapids, Michigan: Eerdmans Publishing Co., 1975.

Farmer, H. H. *The Servant of the Word*. Philadelphia: Fortress Press, 1942.

_____. *The Word of Reconciliation*. Nashville: Abingdon Press, 1966.

Forsyth, P. T. *The Principle of Authority*. 2nd ed. London: Independent Press, 1952.

Fowler, James W., and Lovin, Robin W., Editors. *Trajectories in Faith*. Nashville: Abingdon Press, 1980.

Friedrich, Gerhard, Editor. *Theological Dictionary of the New Testament*. Grand Rapids, Michigan: Eerdmans Publishing Co., 1975.

Fuller, Reginald H. *Made, Not Born*. Notre Dame: University of Notre Dame Press, 1976.

Fung, Raymond. "Evangelism Today." *A Monthly Letter about Evangelism*. The World Council of Churches, July-August, 1979.

Gerkin, Charles V. *Crisis Experience in Modern Life*. Nashville: Abingdon Press, 1979.

"The Gospel Boom." *Saturday Evening Post*. April 1979. Vol. 251.

Green, Bryan. *The Practice of Evangelism*. New York: Charles Scribner's Sons, 1951.

Green, Michael. *Evangelism in the Early Church*. Grand Rapids, Michigan: Eerdmans Publishing Co., 1970.

Hale, Joe. *Design for Evangelism*. Nashville: Tidings, 1969.

_____. Editor. *Proceedings of the 13th World Methodist Conference*. Waynesville, N.C.: Mountaineer Press, 1977.

Hale, J. Russell. *The Unchurched*. San Francisco: Harper and Row, 1980.

Henderson, Robert T. *Joy to the World*. Atlanta: John Knox Press, 1980.

Hendrick, John R. *Opening the Door of Faith*. Atlanta: John Knox Press, 1977.

Hoekendijk, J. C. *The Church Inside Out*. Philadelphia: Westminster Press, 1966.

Holladay, William L. *The Concise Hebrew and Aramaic Lexicon of the Old Testament*. Grand Rapids, Michigan: Eerdmans Publishing Company, 1971.

Holmes, Urban T. III, and Westerhoff, John H. III. *Christian Believing*. New York: Seabury Press, 1979.

Howe, Reuel L. *Man's Need and God's Action*. Greenwich, Connecticut: Seabury Press, 1953.

Hunter, George G. III. *The Contagious Congregation*. Nashville: Abingdon Press, 1979.

_____. Editor. *Focus on Evangelism*. Nashville: Discipleship Resources, 1978.

James, William. *The Varieties of Religious Experience*. New York: Mentor Press, 1958.

Jeremias, Joachim. *Infant Baptism in the First Four Centuries.* London: S.C.M. Press, 1960.

_____. *The Origins of Infant Baptism.* Naperville, Illinois: Alec R. Allenson, Inc., 1963.

Jones, E. Stanley. *Conversion.* New York: Abingdon Press, 1959.

Kasdorf, Hans. *Christian Conversion in Context.* Scottsdale, PA: Herald Press, 1980.

Kavanagh, Aidan. *The Shape of Baptism.* Pueblo: Pueblo Press, 1979.

Keck, Leander. *A Future for the Historical Jesus.* Nashville: Abingdon Press, 1971.

_____. *Mandate to Witness.* Chicago: Judson Press, 1964.

_____. "Theological Themes in Romans." Unpublished manuscript.

Kraus, Norman. *The Authentic Witness.* Grand Rapids, Michigan: Eerdmans Publishing Co., 1979.

Küng, Hans. *Does God Exist?* Translated by Edward Quinn. New York: Doubleday and Co., 1980.

_____. *Justification.* New York: Thomas Nelson and Sons, 1964.

Kurtz, Paul. "Some People Believe Anything They See On T.V." *U. S. News and World Report, Inc.,* May 21, 1979, pp. 52–54.

Laney, James, Editor. *Evangelism: Mandates for Action.* New York: Hawthorne Books, Inc., 1975.

Lewis, C. S. *Surprised by Joy.* New York and London: Harcourt Brace Jovanovich, 1955.

Logan, James C. "The Roots of Our Social Vision." *engage/social action,* December 1979, pp. 10–39.

Luckmann, Thomas. *Invisible Religion.* New York: Macmillan Publishing Co., 1967.

Miller, Keith. *The Becomers.* Waco, Texas: Word Books, 1973.

Moltmann, Jurgen. *The Church in the Power of the Spirit.* New York: Harper and Row Publishers, 1977.

Morris, George. *Shalom.* Nashville: Tidings, 1974.

Newbigin, Leslie. *The Finality of Christ.* London: S.C.M. Press, 1969.

Niles, D. T. *That They May Have Life.* New York: Harper and Brothers, 1951.

Oates, Wayne E. *The Psychology of Religion.* Waco, Texas: Word Books, 1973.

Outler, Albert. *Evangelism in the Wesleyan Spirit.* Nashville: Tidings, 1971.

_____. Editor. *John Wesley.* New York: Oxford University Press, 1964.

_____. *Theology in the Wesleyan Spirit.* Nashville: Tidings, 1975.

Rambo, Lewis R. "Psychological Perspectives on Conversion." *Pacific Theological Review,* XIII (Spring 1980), 21–26.

Reed, Bruce. *The Dynamics of Religion.* London: Darton, Longman & Todd, 1978.

Richardson, Allen Editor. *A Theological Word Book of the Bible.* New York: The Macmillan Co., 1950.

Routley, Erik. *Conversion.* Philadelphia: Fortress Press, 1960.

Runyon, Theodore. "The Finality of Christ." Unpublished manuscript.

———, Editor. *Sanctification and Liberation.* Nashville: Abingdon Press, 1981.

———. "What About Those . . . ?" Unpublished manuscript.

Sargant, William. *Battle for the Mind.* Garden City, New York: Doubleday and Co., Inc., 1957.

Schillebeeckx, Edward. *Christ.* New York: Seabury Press, 1980.

Sherer, Paul. *The Word God Sent.* New York: Harper & Row, 1965.

Shoemaker, Samuel. *How to Become a Christian.* New York: Harper & Row, 1953.

Southard, Samuel. *Pastoral Evangelism.* Nashville: Broadman Press, 1962.

Steinmetz, David C. "Reformation and Conversion." *Theology Today,* XXXV (April 1978), pp. 25/32.

Stott, John R. W. *Christian Mission in the Modern World.* Downer's Grove, Illinois: I.V.P., 1975.

Sweazey, George E. *The Church as Evangelist.* New York: Harper & Row, 1978.

Temple, William. *Christianity and Social Order.* London: S.C.M. Press, 1950.

Tillich, Paul. *Dynamics of Faith.* New York: Harper Colophon Books, 1957.

————. *Systematic Theology.* Vols. I-III. Chicago: University of Chicago Press, 1951–1963.

Tournier, Paul. *The Person Reborn.* London: S.C.M. Press, Ltd., 1966.

Tucker, Gene M. "The Creation and Fall: A Reconsideration." *Lexington Theological Quarterly,* XIII (October 1978), pp. 113–124.

Tuttle, Robert G., Jr. *John Wesley.* Grand Rapids, Michigan: Zondervan Publishing House, 1978.

Wainwright, Geoffrey. *Christian Initiation.* London: Lutterworth Press, 1969.

Walker, Alan. *The New Evangelism.* Nashville: Abingdon Press, 1975.

*The Works of the Rev. John Wesley,* 3rd ed., Edited by Thomas Jackson. 14 vols. London: Wesleyan-Methodist Book Room, 1829–31. Reprinted, Grand Rapids: Zondervan Publishing House, 1958; Grand Rapids: Baker Book House, 1979.

*Wesley's Doctrinal Standards,* Part I. Edited by N. Burwash. Salem, Ohio: Schmul Publishers, 1967 reprint.

*Wesley's Standard Sermons,* Edited by Edward H. Sugden. 2 vols. Reprinted, London: Epworth Press, 1921; 5th ed., 1961.

Westerhoff, John, III. *Will Our Children Have Faith?* New York: Seabury Press, 1976.

Williams, Colin W. *John Wesley's Theology Today.* Nashville: Abingdon Press, 1960.

Wood, A. Skevington. *The Burning Heart.* Minneapolis, Minnesota: Bethany Fellowship, Inc., 1978.